FC

Labour Antise

letters from longstanding Labour members bullied out from their political home by the takeover of the hard left
includes analyses of institutional antisemitism; the intersection of antisemitism and misogyny; timelines and definitions

for link to film FORCED OUT see Facebook group and YouTube

selected and introduced by Judith Ornstein

Kitty Hawk Press Ltd

FORCED OUT

First published Great Britain 2019
By Kitty Hawk Press Ltd
Judith@forcedout.co.uk

To add your resignation letter go to FORCED OUT on Facebook and the excellent but unconnected Twitter account Resignations over antisemitism @resignedfromlab

Thank you to:
All writers included here for giving permission to share your work
Jilly Lester for Kitty Hawk logo
L & L Michaels
J & L Samuel
David Hirsh
Andrea Frankenthal
studiocleanslate.com who designed the cover
concerned individuals who gave generous time and help with this project

And most of all Ged Ornstein
The project is dedicated to our children and grandchildren

'Let me speak to the yet unknowing world how these things came about' Hamlet

A catalogue record for this book is available from the British Library
ISBN 978-1-5272-5339-1

CONTENTS

Part 1 Resignation letters in chronological order

Page

PART 2

INTRODUCTION

'We live together, freely, in a spirit of solidarity, tolerance and respect'
Labour Party Membership Card

These resignation letters have been written by Labour members, Jewish and not. All still hold traditional Labour values but believe they have been traduced by the current leadership. They are principled and brave.
Of the tens of thousands who have walked away from the Labour Party since Jeremy Corbyn became leader, only a few wrote letters. Each included here stands on its own merits, but together the letters establish a testimony providing truthful and moving primary evidence.

EHRC

In May 2019 The Equality and Human Rights Commission launched a formal investigation into allegations of antisemitism in The Labour Party. The only political party previously investigated for racism was the right wing fascist British National Party. Many complaints are made to the EHRC but to proceed they demand the highest evidential bar.
In her resignation letter former MP Bridget Prentice writes:
'That the EHRC feels it needs to investigate the Labour party for antisemitism – an organisation we set up in the face of fury from the right – is

shameful; that women MPs have been bullied out of the party by racists and thugs is shameful; that the leadership continues to fudge on Europe is shameful; that the rules of the party have been changed deny the democracy that so many thought would come with Jeremy is shameful. It is not leadership.'

Dame Louise Ellman MP writes:

'Shamefully, its anti-Jewish racism is now being investigated by one of the last Labour government's proudest creations, the Equality and Human Rights Commission. Jeremy Corbyn – who spent three decades on the backbenches consorting with, and never confronting, antisemites, Holocaust deniers and terrorists – has attracted the support of too many antisemites'

These resignation letters encapsulate how low the Labour Party has sunk since Corbyn took over in 2015.

As former Labour candidate Colin Appleby writes in October 2018:

'I am dismayed at what the Labour Party has become in recent years. We have gone from being a party that could occupy the moral high ground to one that is rotten to the core '

How did this happen?

In 2015 Ed Miliband introduces a £3 membership allowing the public to vote for the next Labour

Party leader. The entryists seize the opportunity and according to the BBC (18th Aug 2015) Labour membership rises to 610,753. The BBC also reports a tidal wave of 160,000 applications in the 24 hours before the deadline.
How could all these people be vetted? The Guardian (20th Aug 2015) suggests that some are more interested in Jeremy Corbyn, who had been a maverick backbencher, than in the Labour Party. The influx of Hard Left extremism is alien to those whose identity is rooted in the values of the UK Labour Party.

Sorrow

The letters are suffused with sorrow, beginning with the first in September 2016 following Corbyn's re-election as Labour Leader, when Lord Parry Mitchell, a one person vanguard, writes: 'with a heavy heart'. Nearly two years later Russell Smith-Becker writes: 'with great sadness'; Frank Field MP: 'with considerable sadness'; former Labour leader of Brighton Council, Warren Morgan 'I despair'; and former Labour deputy leader of Edinburgh City Council Susan Dalgety: 'the Labour Party I loved is dead'
The letter writers are longstanding members; former mayor, Cllr Allan Barclay belonged for 52 years, Fiona Millar, former advisor to both Cherie and Tony Blair, belonged for 40. Richard Horton as chair of Stroud Green CLP; and Russell Smith-Becker, treasurer Islington North CLP, worked locally with Corbyn.

As well as antisemitism, the letters reference: the takeover of Labour by the far left; Brexit; jobs; links to terrorists; anti NATO statements; insults to our armed forces and serious threats to our national security.

Allan Barclay speaks for many: ‘As an Armed Forces veteran I fear the Labour Party is at a dark turning point and marching towards fascism at a steady pace. I have witnessed antisemitism, racism, homophobia, disability discrimination and a general disrespect towards others.’

The letters chronicle degeneration in the Labour Party culture under Corbyn.

Mike Gapes MP writes ‘I care passionately about traditional Labour values of fairness, social justice, equality and internationalism’ but he continues: ‘This is not the Labour Party I joined or have supported for so many years.’

Fiona Millar calls it ‘the nasty, cultish, sectarian, “with us or against us” streak in Corbyn’s Labour.’

Colin illustrates just that: ‘I’ve been told “shut up Jew” when I’ve voiced an unpopular opinion.’

Here’s councillor Merilyn Davies: ‘I have been told I am being paid by Israel, that I support the murder of Palestinian children, I am unhinged, a liar, deceitful’

The abuse continues when people leave.

Fiona again: ‘A short tweet on the subject of my membership dilemma early this week elicited the usual “piss off then” response from supporters of the current leadership’

The vituperation escalates with Richard's evidence. After resigning 'At the very next branch meeting I was described as having had a "breakdown" and that I was "mentally unstable". This was nothing more than gaslighting.' Richard describes the reaction to Russell's resignation by those 'claiming to be your (Corbyn's) supporters on Facebook. Much of it was conspiratorial and some of it was overtly antisemitic. He was told to "f*** off", accused of resigning to prevent criticism of Israel and asked how he would spend his "thirty pieces of silver"'

Misogyny

Each letter talks of antisemitism but it turns even more sinister when directed at women. In February 2019 Luciana Berger MP resigns from the party when she is targeted with antisemitic and violent misogyny by those claiming to be Corbyn supporters, Although it is unremitting the party apparatus neither protects her nor informs her of a death threat. The invective aimed at Joan Ryan MP and Dame Louise Ellman MP is just as vicious and yet, even in the wake of the tragic murder of Jo Cox MP, Labour's response is to deny and obfuscate. Here are two examples from Richard's letter: 'The threats made by your (Corbyn's) supporters to Luciana Berger's unborn child. The threat by one of your supporters to Joan Ryan that she should be 'shoved right back in the ovens.'

Examples of Labour's denial and obfuscation are on p. 193

The toxic combination of antisemitism and misogyny is analysed by Dr David Hirsh p. 179 and Dr Lesley Klaff p.185.

By August 2018 Cllr Frances Weetman is the first to hint that the unchecked Jew hate goes deeper than a slew of individual incidents. Frances explains why, like so many others, she has waited before resigning:

'As long as the party's processes are sound, I originally reasoned, then there is no reason to leave. Any political movement has its fair share of cranks. As long as the party has the wherewithal and desire to act appropriately, then all is not lost.'

Rather than include his original letter of resignation from 2017, the only one I could find from that year, Dr Daniel Allington decided to reflect on his own journey out of the party. The integrity and insight of his contribution to FORCED OUT on p. 166 will resonate with many.

Institutional antisemitism

Most of these courageous and engrossing resignation letters start in 2018 but it's former UJS chair Hannah Rose alone who, in September that year, is clear sighted and brave enough to use the 'I' word:

'I cannot give support or succour to a party which its own MPs consider to be institutionally racist.'

Nobody in this selection specifies institutional Jew hate again until 2019 when former Labour cllr Adam Langleben, David Hirsh, Cllr Rowan Draper, Richard Horton, Merilyn Davies and cllr Jason Fotjik all accuse Labour of institutional antisemitism.

Adam says:

'You (Jeremy Corbyn), Seumas Milne, Karie Murphy, Len McClusky, the bullies at the top have all allowed this culture of institutionalised antisemitism to develop and grow. You have fed a culture of denial that has allowed this sickness to spread. You brief Alt-Left media such as Skwawkbox, which disseminates your message to distrust Jews en masse.'

Russell addresses Corbyn: 'When I encouraged you to take swift action on antisemitism I meant against it rather than to increase tolerance of it.'

Rowan adds: 'The election of Jeremy Corbyn as Leader of the Labour Party, along with the transformation of the party, has meant that the party has descended into the sewer. It is now a safe-haven for antisemites'

Here's Lord David Triesman in July 2019: 'My sad conclusion is that the Labour Party is very plainly institutionally antisemitic, and its leader and his circle are antisemitic having never once made the right judgement call about an issue reflecting deep prejudice. The number of examples is shocking'

Dr Eve Garrard is a moral philosopher with a special interest in the Holocaust. She explains institutional antisemitism on p. 170 with wisdom and lucidity.

Jews not welcome There's sadness but no surprise in Richard's letter, March 2019:

'Over the past eighteen months, slowly but surely, all of my Jewish friends have left Labour'

Hannah writes: 'the party has made clear through its actions that I am not welcome' and David Hirsh finishes his letter 'I'm done. And I think most other Jews are done too'.

On p. 200 is a concise timeline of events leading up to this crisis.

Corbyn takes over Labour in September 2015 and with him arrive those who Jew bait and who say and do antisemitic things. Even if people are disciplined there's a tendency to let them back in unobtrusively.

In February 2016 there is evidence of antisemitism in Oxford University Labour Club but Baroness Royall's report is suppressed.

June 2016 sees the publication of the **Chakrabarti Report**. Bridget Prentice: 'The whitewash that was the Chakrabarti Report should have been a signal that this leadership was either incapable of leading or prepared to accept racists and bullies as long as they were their racists and bullies'

Joan Ryan pithily describes Corbynism's inadequacy in tackling antisemitism: 'it has offered white-wash reports. It has operated a revolving door disciplinary policy with those accused of antisemitism briefly suspended and then quietly readmitted to the party. And it has allowed its surrogates to belittle the scale of the problem and attack those who try to bring it to light.'

You can find primary evidence about the failings of the Chakrabarti Report from those who wrote submissions but were ignored in The Whitewashed project, book available on Amazon.co.uk and film on YouTube. Links also on www.whitewashed.co.uk.

Proof of the report's inadequacy is that three and a half years after its publication the party is undergoing an EHRC inquiry.

Existential threat to Jewish Life On 25th July 2018 The Jewish Chronicle, The Jewish News and The Jewish Telegraph run this headline across their front pages about a potential Corbyn government. On Friday 3rd August, at 17.30 on the eve of the Jewish Shabbat when no orthodox Jew is allowed to respond, Jeremy Corbyn decides to answer back. It's in the Guardian and doesn't start too badly, but in the third paragraph he refers to the headlines as 'overheated rhetoric.' Again Corby promises to speed up the processing of cases yet fifteen months later, before December 2019's general election Labour is standing candidates with a history of saying or endorsing antisemitic things.

Despite Corbyn's assertion to the contrary on ITV leadership debate Nov 2019 it is claimed that there is still a backlog of disciplinary cases, some going back years.

In the same Guardian article Corbyn references what he calls 'few' examples of antisemitism within the party, thereby demonstrating no comprehension of institutional racism.

Jews have always argued Jeremy Corbyn and his circle, have attempted to exploit how Jews wrangle. Yes - it's in our DNA. People in the Corbyn cult love Jewish Voice for Labour, and this tiny antizionist splinter group reciprocates.

Richard Horton explains why JVL is one of the reasons he's resigned:

'Instead of listening to the concerns raised by Jewish Labour Movement delegates and local Rabbis, Hornsey and Wood Green CLP then voted overwhelmingly in favour of "affiliating" to Jewish Voice for Labour. It seemed a deliberately provocative act towards our local Jewish community.

Paradoxically Corbyn has drawn us closer. An October 2019 Jewish Chronicle survey reveals that 93 percent of UK's Jews won't vote for Labour under Corbyn. This figure is identical to a 2015 survey revealing that 93 percent of UK Jews regard Israel as part of their identity. This confirms that most of us know, as Lord Leslie Turnberg says, that 'Antizionism has become the new antisemitism'.

In her letter Judith Flacks- Leigh writes 'the Jewish community does have more in common than that which divides us, and that is why the tactic of trying to exploit our divisions will not work...... I cannot be part of a Labour Party that tries to exploit divisions in a community to divert away from a conversation about racism'

There's an old joke about a Jew stranded on a desert island who builds two synagogues because he's fallen out with the first. Corbynist tactics backfire because they have (sort of) united us. This is exemplified by the three Jewish newpapers' headline. And it is spectacularly on show in the letter of 16th July 2018 condemning Labour antisemitism and signed, without precedent, by 68 Rabbis, across all strands of Judaism. It's on record on p. 205

Integrity I believe that the letter writers in this book speak for many people of conscience who could not be bystanders; they were forced out despite doing their utmost to stand by the values stated on the Labour Party membership card. They may have stopped paying their dues; written a one liner; or, like Tracey Ann Oberman who, after Ken Livingstone wasn't expelled, tweeted at Labour: 'Like so many of us whose East End heritage was steeped in Labour, I'm reeling today. Resigning my membership. Feel so let down.

Finally, here are Richard Horton and Adam Langleben.

Richard: 'how can I 'teach my daughter about what Anne Frank endured and her legacy if I remain a member of an institutionally anti-Semitic political party? I would be a hypocrite if I did. The only decent thing to do is for me to resign.'

Adam to Jeremy Corbyn: 'One day my son may ask me what I did to stop you from ever becoming Prime Minister. I can no longer look my family and friends in the face without complete shame. Well this is something small, but I will no longer be part of this. I will no longer pay subscriptions to an antisemitic movement. I will sign one pledge and that is to stop a party led by antisemites from ever gaining power in this country and I will continue to live by the values on the back of my now torn up membership card'.

21st September 2016
Lord Parry Mitchell

Dear Angela
I will be leaving the party and will be doing so with a heavy heart - I will resign at the weekend. Steve, Toby as well as yourself have made very strong points, as have others. You say that the Labour Peers are the only group who can hold this Government to account: this is undeniable. You say that we will continue to plough our own furrow: that is also true. Finally you say that every loss of a Labour Parliamentarian is a victory for the bad guys - sadly that too is correct.
If it were for those reasons alone I'd be hanging on, albeit through gritted teeth - the fact is that it is much more.
First of all there are major policy areas where I strongly disagree with the leadership. Business, NATO, Trident, EU etc - these are passionate issues for me and I would find it hard to be part of a party where the leaders sit on the other side of the fence.
But secondly and most critically is the antisemitism and antizionism that emanate from the Leader's office. As a Jew and a firm supporter of the State of Israel (for all its faults) I as an individual cannot be a member of a party whose leadership is so vehement in its hatred.
Half of Jan's report on anti-semitism was censored by the NEC and even worse Shami's

report was a whitewash - a slap on the wrist for offenders where a lifetime ban was what should have been recommended.

I am a fighter by nature: I will slug it out with the best of them, but this fight has been lost and as Neil so eloquently put it 'there will be no Labour Government in our lifetimes'

My decision is very distressing - the Labour Peers Group have become my political family - it has not been taken lightly. But I loathe Corbyn and his pals - I want to have nothing more to do with them.

I have also decided not to slip away quietly into the night - I would see that as the cowards way out. People will ask questions and I need to give truthful answers.

After Conference I am happy to go over the mechanics.

You are my friends and I will miss sitting amongst you.

Lord Parry Mitchell

20th April 2018
Judith Flacks-Leigh
Judith's resignation was an open letter in The Jewish News

Last night, I decided with a heavy heart, to terminate my Labour Party membership and end my participation in the Jo Cox Women in Leadership programme.
I have watched over the last two years as the Labour Party that I know and love has deteriorated in to a space where antisemites feel welcome, can be openly antisemitic, and face no consequences. The few that have been suspended or expelled have undergone drawn out, unnecessarily long processes to reach that conclusion. Many cases of reported antisemitism haven't even been looked in to. I have sat, excruciatingly patiently, waiting for the Leadership of the Party to act faster, do more than talk about front bench personal records of fighting racism while continuing to ignore antisemitism.
I stayed with the Labour Party when many of my Jewish friends and family left, feeling it was no longer a safe space for them. I stayed, believing that one should stay and fight for what they believe in, and really believing that this neglect to deal with antisemitism would change.
I submitted verbal evidence to the Chakrabarti inquiry, and told Shami, face to face, of the

experiences I have had and how uncomfortable it is to read the word "antisemitism" sprawled across the front pages of the newspapers and appear on headline news, and to sit there thinking "they're talking about my religion. What does that reader think? Do they agree? Are they antisemitic? Do they think I'm making it up? Or do they get it?" I read Shami part of my father's Labour Party membership resignation letter, and she said she would respond. Of course, two years later, he has seen nothing from either her or our MP, who he also wrote to, voicing his concerns about antisemitism in the party. After 30 years of loyal party membership, he deserved more.

But still, I stayed. I stayed, and I kept saying that this would all pass and that soon, the leadership would wake up and finally get it. I wish "naïve" was all that I have been called for believing this. To be called a "Kapo" by some (for those reading this who don't know, Kapos were prisoners, often Jewish, in Nazi concentration camps who were assigned by SS guards to supervise forced labour or worse), for staying in the party, is a wound that will cut deeper than many will be able to understand.

I still stayed. I applied for the Jo Cox Women in Leadership programme, which has taught me a lot about self-confidence, about support and about female leaders and leadership, and I have met some wonderful women through it who will make great councillors, MPs and leaders when they are given the chance. And it is almost because of this programme, that I feel like I have reached a limit.

This week, after agreeing that there would be a meeting with the JLC and Board of Deputies to discuss antisemitism in the party and how to move forward, a number of people in the Jewish community from a whole host of contentious and mainstream organisations, received emails from the Leader's office inviting them to a round table to discuss the same thing the next day.

By doing this, the Leader's office are trying again, as they previously had done with Jeremy Corbyn's attendance at the Jewdas seder, to turn the attention from antisemitism in the Labour Party, to infighting and fractures in the Jewish community. For a brief moment two weeks ago, that tactic worked and the news stories were no longer purely about antisemitism, but about who the "establishment" accepted was part of the Jewish community.

To use the same tactic again is something I cannot stand for. I will not be part of a party who peddle the line "we have more in common than that which divides us", whilst they quite literally seek to exaggerate and highlight the divisions in the Jewish community to divert the conversation away from dealing with antisemitism. No other community in this country would be treated this way by a mainstream political party. Encouraging in-fighting and highlighting divisions to discredit, undermine and divert serious conversations about antisemitism. This is a tactic straight out of a 1930s Germany play-book, and I cannot and will not be part of a party that uses that tactic against a religious minority. Against my community. Against my religion. Against me.

These divisions that the party think they are highlighting and exploiting don't make us weaker. Our diversity makes us stronger. Our differences are something that we cherish. We come from all kinds of backgrounds, from all over the world, from all different socio-economic backgrounds, and we have a huge diversity of opinion on politics. We are not homogeneous.

But the Jewish community does have more in common than that which divides us, and that is why the tactic of trying to exploit our divisions will not work.

The Labour Party will have to deal with antisemitism at some stage. I hope, for its own sake, and for the sake of the many people in this country who desperately need a Labour government, that it does it soon so that it can one day truly be a party for the many, not the few. But until that day, I cannot be part of a Labour Party that tries to exploit divisions in a community to divert away from a conversation about racism.

Judith Flacks-Leigh

18th July 2018
John Woodcock
Member of Parliament Barrow and Furness 2010-2019

Jeremy Corbyn
Leader of the Labour Party

Dear Jeremy,
I am today resigning from the Labour Party following your refusal to appoint an independent investigator to rule on my disciplinary case and in the light of clear evidence that the process has been manipulated for factional purposes.
First and foremost let me make clear that I was elected to put the people of Barrow and Furness first, no matter how difficult or controversial. I have promised to fight for local jobs, promote a credible alternative government, protect the shipyard and ensure the safety of my constituents through strong defence and national security. I now believe more strongly than ever that you have made the Labour Party unfit to deliver those objectives and would pose a clear risk to UK national security as prime minister.
The party for which I have campaigned since I was a boy is no longer the broad church it has always historically been. Antisemitism is being tolerated and Labour has been taken over at nearly every level by the hard left, far beyond the dominance they achieved at the height of 1980s militancy.

There is little chance of returning the Labour Party to the inclusive, mainstream electoral force my constituents desperately need. In these circumstances, I can no longer justify engaging in a rigged process to be re-admitted to it. As you know, Labour's new general secretary, who has previously said she wanted to 'ditch Blairites', overturned a previous ruling of a party disciplinary panel and suspended me after someone placed confidential details of my disciplinary case in two Sunday newspapers. This followed a newspaper report that the Labour leadership was looking for a reason to suspend me because of my opposition to your leadership. Emails that have since been released to me through data laws reveal that senior party figures have long been determined to prevent me re-standing as a Labour candidate because of my views on your leadership. It was noted in one such email that suspending me for a reason unrelated to those views would enable me to be barred from re-selection without risking legal challenge.

It is not credible to expect a fair hearing in these circumstances. I strongly deny the charge made against me but am committed to the complaint being thoroughly and fairly investigated. I will now seek to refer myself to an independent process so the case can be properly heard. I hope you will listen to the growing calls from the

Labour Too campaign and others to do the same for all cases.

I am proud of what our community has achieved since I was given the opportunity to serve them in parliament, despite damaging government austerity. We have secured the historic Trident vote that guarantees two decades of work in Barrow shipyard; we have saved our maternity unit; and we are coming together to demand promised new investment to lift the crippling deprivation that blights too many local lives.

There is still so much to do and I will continue to give my all to the people of Barrow and Furness as an independent MP on the opposition benches. My loyalty to them always comes first so I will work with the government when it is trying to do the right thing, and will also work with the many good colleagues who are still trying to do their best in Labour.

John Woodcock

24 July 2018
Councillor Russell Smith-Becker
Former treasurer Islington North CLP

Rt Hon Jeremy Corbyn MP
House of Commons
24 July 2018

Dear Jeremy
<u>Resignation from the Labour Party</u>
As you know, I have been an active member of the Labour Party for many years. It has been a big part of my life, and as well as hundreds of hours of door-knocking I have had numerous positions in the party. I was for several years your constituency treasurer in Islington North, and for several years the Secretary of Islington's Local Campaign Forum (previously Local Government Committee) – this time last year I was dealing with the big tasks of getting all potential Islington Council candidates interviewed and the administration of the wards' shortlisting and selection meetings.
It is therefore with great sadness that I write this letter. It is a real wrench to leave the party I have been a member of for 28 years (my entire adult life – I joined before I could vote).I last wrote to you on 26 March, just after attending the demonstration about antisemitism in the Labour Party organised by the Jewish Leadership Council (JLC) and the Board of Deputies of British Jews

(BoD), after your Facebook comments on the antisemitic mural surfaced.

In a public letter you wrote to those organisations at the time and also in your reply to me you acknowledged the problem of antisemitism in the party and the pain it has caused, saying that it has 'often been dismissed as simply a matter of a few bad apples'. As you have acknowledged this I don't need to go through what would be a lengthy list of antisemitic incidents in the party.

You said that you will be a militant opponent of antisemitism and that you wanted to talk with Jewish organisations about this. In my letter to you I urged you to act swiftly and convincingly.

So, what has happened since then?

Ken Livingstone remained a member of the party until he chose to resign, despite the longstanding complaints against him. You said that his resignation was 'sad'.

Jackie Walker remains a member of the party.

Chris Williamson has continued to defend and share platforms with various people who are subject to complaints of antisemitism. That MPs not be permitted to do this was one of the key demands of the JLC and BoD. Williamson still has the Labour whip.

A great number of other complaints of antisemitism have not been dealt with and those people remain party members.

Christine Shawcroft, then the chair of the Disputes Sub-Committee, was revealed to have supported a member who had shared a Holocaust denial post. She said that she had not seen this image but that if she had she would have sent the member for antisemitism training. Despite being the chair of the Disputes Sub-Committee she thought that this was sufficient for Holocaust denial (the nature of the training wasn't explained, but perhaps it would include 'actually the Holocaust did happen'). Shawcroft eventually resigned from the NEC but her original actions say something about how normalised the tolerance of antisemitism has become in the party.

In April, The Sunday Times reported that it had uncovered over 2,000 examples of antisemitic, racist, violent threats and abusive content in non-public Corbyn-supporting Facebook groups, including frequent attacks on Jews and Holocaust denying material.

Lord Sugar made a racist tweet. Dawn Butler (rightly) criticised him for this, but felt the need to remind everybody that he is Jewish. She did not apologise for this, but remained on the front bench.

The NEC has recently decided to water down the International Holocaust Remembrance Alliance (IHRA) definition of antisemitism by not including all of its examples of antisemitism.

We both know that the full IHRA definition allows criticism of Israel and its government so there is no reason to water down for that purpose.

The argument made by some for the watering down is that that it focuses on the reason for an antisemitic statement, so that people are only suspended or expelled if they are motivated by hatred of Jews. I don't know how valid this argument is, but if it is valid then anyone can defend themselves by saying 'yes I did say those things but I wasn't motivated by antisemitism'. Some have said that in practice removing those examples would not much change the effect of the overall definition because they are covered by text elsewhere in the definition. Maybe they are right, but it is still a watering down. If the response from the NEC to the problem of antisemitism in the Labour party is that we are being too strict in disciplining it then this is the wrong direction of travel, and contrary to what you said in March when you acknowledged the problem and said you wanted to deal with it. As Ann Black said in her recent NEC report: *This is no longer about technical niceties, or who is wrong and who is right in a court of law, but about trust. My view is that the only way back from the brink is to rise above the trenches, reiterate our commitment to the full IHRA paper and, where necessary, elaborate its provisions within the code. No other organisation adopting IHRA has sought to separate the two-sentence definition from the examples, and it is hard to explain why Labour, alone, has to do so. The examples are just*

examples, and Labour's own NCC would interpret them within their context.
Unlike some of the other bullet points above, which are not the responsibility of you or the NEC, or which are but might be blamed on incompetence, mistake or mis-prioritisation, this is a specific decision by the NEC. <u>A decision to be less tough on antisemitism.</u> This is after you acknowledged back in March that there is a significant problem of antisemitism in the party and said you would act against it and (as evidenced by the bullet points) the situation has got worse since.
I was perhaps unclear in my previous letter to you on this topic. When I encouraged you to listen to the JLC, BoD and other community groups I meant with a view to doing as they ask rather than the opposite. When I encouraged you to take swift action on antisemitism I meant against it rather than to increase tolerance of it.
You have said that you are not antisemitic and I believe you. Merely saying this is not enough though – if you are so often tolerant towards antisemitism then this has the same practical effect as if you were antisemitic, and it is hardly surprising that people like Margaret Hodge might get the impression that you are.

You are the leader of the party and should be providing leadership on this, but it's not just about the party. Would you fight antisemitism if

you were the Prime Minister, or would you ask the numerous public bodies which use the IHRA definition of antisemitism to dilute it?
A common suggestion made (typically by people who do not believe that antisemitism exists in the party) is that those complaining about it are doing so not because of the antisemitism itself but because of discontent on the way the party has moved in other areas since you became leader. That is certainly not the case with me. I have a range of concerns about how the party has changed (for example the half-hearted campaigning against Brexit in advance of the referendum; the sometimes unthinking support for the governments of Venezuela and Russia; members who rubbish the 'Mainstream Media' while accepting what is in the Canary or RT). On the other hand I could write a list of changes I agree with - the 2017 manifesto was one which I could get behind, and I was pleased that you grasped the nettle on some issues (such as the arms trade) not grasped by previous leaders. Other than the tolerance of antisemitism, the things I disagree with are all things I would have been prepared to stay in the party and hope to influence on from within. I am happy to support a party which is a force for good even if I have some differences, but I am no longer sure that the Labour party is a force for good.
I therefore resign my membership of the Labour Party. The Labour Party has become somewhere

where antisemites feel comfortable and where many Jews feel uncomfortable – I hope I can join again when it is the other way around.

Councillor Russell Smith-Becker

4th August 2018
Fiona Millar
Journalist and campaigner on education and *parenting issues; former advisor to Cherie and Tony Blair.*

Fiona sent a short resignation email to the Labour Party shortly after writing this open letter in the Observer 4th August 2018

For 40 years I've stayed with the party, dark days and all. Why am I now on the brink of leaving? Every morning is the same now: wake up, read the papers, start the internal dialogue about how much longer Labour party membership is bearable. Reading that sentence back, it looks ridiculously melodramatic. No one has died and millions of people exist perfectly happily without membership of any political party. Lucky them. But for those of us who have spent decades (in my case more than 40 years) as members of Labour, these are not easy times. I grew up in a strictly atheist household, where the party was akin to religion. My parents were products of the trade union-sponsored Ruskin College; my father worked on Tribune in the 1950s. My childhood was punctuated by Labour events: Saturday mornings churning out newsletters on an ancient Gestetner copier, Labour bazaars, election campaigns and ward meetings.

Becoming, at 16, assistant party secretary in the high-Tory constituency of St Marylebone (the secretary was the Dowager Lady Lucan, no less), was a thankless task, politically. But friendships were formed which remain strong today. The sense of common endeavour and solidarity, regardless of political disagreements, is a powerful memory.

I stayed with hope and confidence through the "dark days" of the early 1980s, lived through the foundation of the SDP, worked at the heart of the first Labour government for 18 years, saw the many strengths and some weakness of New Labour at close quarters, and endured disagreements and disappointments over Iraq and aspects of Blair/Brown education policy. But I never seriously contemplated quitting, and still consider the opportunity to serve a Labour prime minister a great privilege.

So why now? The most pressing reason is Brexit. If there is an election in the next 12 months, I won't be able to vote for a party that supports or facilitates Brexit. Although Jeremy Corbyn's speeches on the subject are rare, the latest was unequivocal: "Labour Brexit" can be a good thing for the UK. I profoundly disagree. It is against the party rules to vote against official candidates, so it would be dishonest to do so.

But Brexit isn't the only reason. The shockingly badly handled antisemitism row has exposed yet again the nasty, cultish, sectarian, "with us or against us" streak in Corbyn's Labour that sits ill with the party's longstanding, comradely tolerance of difference, which included Corbyn's numerous Commons rebellions.

I am conflicted at leaving behind stalwart members of my local party, now doomed to endure long wars of attrition.

A short tweet on the subject of my membership dilemma early this week elicited the usual "piss off then" response from supporters of the current leadership. Labour MP Ben Bradshaw shot back: "Don't leave – that is what they want." But what have we come to, supporting a party that actively wants members to leave and appears happy to deter potential voters? Elections are usually won by winning over people who previously didn't agree with you, not by displacing those who did.

The turmoil of the past few weeks – much of which could easily have been avoided by a swift admission (or at least in Friday's Guardian article) that it was a mistake not to adopt the internationally recognised definition of antisemitism – has also exposed something many of us fear. That Corbyn is completely unsuited to being prime minister.

It is not just the people he surrounds himself with, several of whom were not even in the party when he became leader. It's that he appears to be unable to hear opposing arguments or seek compromise, and is so sanctimoniously sure of himself that he is prepared to countenance

possible terminal damage to the party's fortunes. Why should his leadership of the country be any different?
Finally, to me anyway, he isn't even very radical. I have searched in vain for any far-reaching ideas that might disrupt our current market-driven, hierarchical school system – my particular area of interest. But there are none. Without drastic change to current education policy Corbyn's banal rhetoric about fairness and equality is just hot air.
So why am I still here? The truth is, it is a wrench to leave. Many Labour MPs are my friends, and I am conflicted about the thought of leaving behind stalwart members of my local party, who are now doomed to endure long wars of attrition over petty interpretations of arcane rules with people who appear to hate members of their own tribe more than they do the Tories. "I am not going to let them steal my party," one told me. Unfortunately, my deepest and most unpleasant suspicion is that they already have, and we won't be getting it back any time soon. All the main institutions – the party HQ, the national executive committee and the leader's office – are in the hands of the intolerant, blinkered hard left. This is unprecedented. If the party rules change dramatically, as is predicted, it won't be like the 1980s; this time the fight might be in vain.
But I still find it hard to visualise phoning Labour membership services and uttering the words, "I want to cancel my membership." About 1% of me

is waiting for a sign that something will change: a climbdown on antisemitism; the powerful Momentum grouping realising the cult of Corbyn is doomed and seeking a leadership election; a more inclusive approach to moderate members; or, above all, a recognition that Labour's best interests, and those of the most vulnerable in society, are served by opposing Brexit.

Even at this late stage, I know my predicament isn't unique. After seeing my tweet last week, many people contacted me in private and public to say they had already quit. One old friend and fellow education campaigner observed: "If you are thinking like that, you have left already."

If your political home is where your heart is, that may well be true.

Fiona Millar

6th August 2018
Councillor Frances Weetman

Dear Sir/Madam,
I have spent 8 years as a dedicated Labour activist, working across multiple CLPs and, since 2016, as a Labour Councillor. I joined the Labour Party at the age of 18, keen to fight for social justice and for an anti-racist, socialist government that protects the rights of minorities. Today, I have decided that these aims are incompatible with my membership of the Labour Party. I write to resign my membership, and by extension the Labour whip.
I firmly believe that the solutions to inequality and disadvantage lie in socialist government. Disadvantage comes in many forms, economic and cultural and racial. I echo JK Rowling when I say that underlying my politics is the principle that it should not matter what a person is born, but what they grow up to be. My anti-racism goes hand-in-hand with my socialism. I sadly see too much evidence that Jeremy Corbyn does not hold the same principles.
Continuing support for the Labour Party, as an anti-racist, would require that I overlook too many of the Leader's actions. Corbyn's supporters routinely opine that his behaviour is the product of his passionate support of Palestine. To claim this is to do Corbyn a disservice. Corbyn has spent a forty-year political

career actively surrounding himself with Holocaust deniers, pursuing policies that emphasise that the *Holocaust didn't just kill Jews*, and making unhelpful comparisons between Israeli government policy and the Holocaust. He has routinely dismissed Jewish concerns about antisemitism. In a 2015 Vice documentary, he labelled accusations of antisemitism in Labour "subliminal nastiness." It is possible to fight for the plight of the Palestinians without doing any of these things. In fact, he tarnishes the reputation of pro-Palestine movements through his actions. No level of naïvety can account for his political choices. This is a man who willingly received Iranian money in 2012 to appear on the country's government propaganda channel, and used this platform not to denounce the oppression of the Iranian people, but to claim ISIS attacks in Egypt were committed by Israel. His recent article in The Guardian (Friday 3rd August 5.30pm) was an affront to anyone concerned by his actions, or by antisemitism within the party: it conceded no ground regarding the IHRA definition, and made no attempt to explain his problematic political history. It dismissed the concerns of a community who, less than 100 years ago, were subject to genocide, as "overheated rhetoric." It was a non-apology, callously posted as the Shabbat began, allowing no response from the observant Jewish community. Jeremy Corbyn knew what he was doing in 2012, and he knows what he is doing now. It would be an insult to his intelligence to claim otherwise.

As a Labour representative, I would be required to defend the actions of the Leader to voters. Councillors, and other elected representatives, are surely treated as fools when we are expected to posit on the doorstep that Corbyn is not an antisemite. I would be expected, I presume, to portray as an accident that the Labour leader defended a mural depicting hook-nosed men crushing bodies while controlling the New World Order. On this basis, it is also an accident that, in 2011, Corbyn signed a Parliamentary motion that aimed to remove the word "Holocaust" from the moniker "Holocaust Memorial Day". An accident, too, that the Labour leader organised an event on Holocaust Memorial Day *with the express purpose* of comparing the actions of modern-day Israel to the systematic, mechanised murder of six million Jews under the Nazis. I will not patronise the electorate by claiming that Corbyn is an unlucky victim of circumstance. These things are not accidents. Nor are they simply insensitive: their aim is erasure of recent Jewish history. His supporters' continued defence of him shows they have a level of chutzpah I daresay I envy.

I do believe the Labour Party is more than its leader. One of the reasons I have remained a member so long is that I cannot bear the thought that I would leave the party - which has been at the forefront of the fight for social justice for a century - to the minority of bad people. Every good, concerned member that leaves reduces the proportion of good, concerned members in the party at large. The antisemitism in the party comes from a minority of members, a fringe of a movement that contains well-meaning people. But this is a fringe that, strikingly, seems to have control of the leadership and the party's processes.

As long as the Party's processes are sound, I originally reasoned, then there is no reason to leave. Any political movement has its fair share of cranks. As long as the Party has the wherewithal and desire to act appropriately, then all is not lost. But the evidence is that the processes no longer serve the minorities they ought to protect.

It is revealing that Margaret Hodge - a lifelong anti-racist campaigner, who fought the BNP in her constituency - was subject to a disciplinary investigation less than a day after she attempted to hold our leader to account. By contrast, Pete Willsman still faces no recompense. In my hometown of Newcastle, a councillor has been permitted to re-stand for election as a Labour candidate, despite denying planning permission to M&S on the grounds that the company was founded by "Zionists who murder Palestinians". The Labour Party's disciplinary process regarding antisemitism seems at best incompetent, and at worst deliberately one-sided. As soon as any organisation's processes fall to prejudice, or racism, then it is strikingly difficult to make any significant change. I fear the changes needed to combat racism will never happen.

The first of these changes must be the implementation of the IHRA definition of antisemitism, in full, with all examples in their original form. It seems important to note that the IHRA definition explicitly permits criticism of Israel. From the outside, it seems that the rewording of the IHRA definition may have been driven by a desire to protect Labour members - possibly including individuals in the Leadership - from criticism. Corbyn's 2010 meeting on Holocaust Memorial Day could, I imagine, be labelled as antisemitic under the full definition. If protecting individuals *is* the motivation, then this shows that the Labour Party currently prioritises electoral and financial gain over any genuine desire to combat prejudice. The NEC has, I believe, indicated through its decision that the Jewish community is the only minority not permitted to define the discrimination it faces.

In 1929 the Wall Street Crash caused a global financial crisis. Ten years later, fascism spread across Europe and caused the outbreak of war. The latest economic downturn began just over ten years ago, in 2007. Nationalism and racism has, again, reared its ugly head, in the UK and abroad. I fear we have not learnt enough from the lessons of history. I cannot remain a member

of, or help fund, an organisation that I feel is complicit in prejudice.
I leave not because I have abandoned Labour values, but because I feel the Party has.

With sadness and regret

Councillor Frances Weetman

4th September 2018
Susan Dalgety
Scotsman columnist and a former deputy leader of Edinburgh City Council
Open Letter, Scotsman

Why I have decided to quit Labour party after 38 years

I am leaving the Labour Party, the organisation that has been a huge part of my life since I joined, as a young mother, in 1980.
I met my husband through the party, made lifelong friends, worked for a Labour First Minister. I was even lucky enough to be a Labour councillor for seven years on Edinburgh City Council.
I marched behind Labour banners, delivered countless leaflets, cried at election results, especially in 1997 when we won that famous landslide. I was Labour for life ... or so I thought.
Then came Saturday, 12 September 2015.
As Jeremy Corbyn was announced as leader of our party, I turned to my husband, and said, through tears: "Well, our party has just been subject of a hostile takeover ... we are finished."
And so it has turned out. The hostile takeover is complete. An unlikely coalition of grumpy old blokes in Lenin caps and wide-eyed millennials in Converse, aided and abetted by some sinister

apparatchiks, now controls our party. The numbers are against us.

I have no heart to go over the reasons I am leaving – there are too many – but in the final analysis it boils down to this: the Labour Party I loved is dead.

I am not antisemitic, I am not pro-Brexit and I don't believe a command economy will work in Britain. And I am no longer a member of the Labour Party.

I have no intention of joining another party. I am still Labour, always will be. At its best, the party has transformed our country and improved people's lives beyond measure, from the NHS to devolution.

But the party has changed beyond recognition, it is now the plaything of self-confessed Stalinists, former Trotskyists and failed playground revolutionaries.

At a time when our country needs the best possible opposition to win the best possible Brexit deal and so protect our economy, the Labour Party is tearing itself apart over whether its leader is a racist. That is shameful.

It is one of the toughest decisions I have ever made, but in the end one of the easiest. I just couldn't stomach it anymore.

Susan Dalgety

12th September 2018
Hannah Rose
Former member, Hertsmere CLP and Bristol Labour Students, and president of the Union of Jewish Students

To Jennie Formby,
General Secretary, Labour Party

Dear Ms Formby,
It is with sincere regret that I write to you today to resign my membership of the Labour Party. My position as the President of the Union of Jewish Students means I cannot, in good faith, continue as a member of a political party which has deliberately and recklessly allowed antisemitism to emerge, and even more concerningly, flourish. I commend the efforts of many Jewish students who stay and fight for the party I still wish I could call my political home. However, both in my personal and professional capacity, I cannot give support or succour to a party which its own MPs consider to be institutionally racist.
I did not join the Labour Party to watch racism against Jews make headlines every single day. I joined to aid the plight of refugees in Europe and tackle the mental health crisis in our youth. These are causes that the Union of Jewish Students will be championing during my Presidency, following

my election on a mandate of social justice and representation. These are the causes that are meant to also drive the Labour Party, but instead it seems more concerned with a battle between internal factions, rather than fighting for the very values it was founded on.

The party's complete inability and lack of political will to tackle antisemitism, whether malicious or simply misguided, has rendered itself a shell of what Her Majesty's Opposition should be.

The period between the Jewish New Year, Rosh Hashanah, and the Day of Atonement, Yom Kippur, is traditionally a period for reflection and repentance. We look back at the past year, and forward to the year to come, and consider how we can better ourselves and the world around us. After a summer of rampant antisemitism in the Labour Party, a constant string of headlines and a debilitating online conversation surrounding Jewish people in this country, I have arrived at a point where I cannot see my future in this party. However, I must take this opportunity to thank those who are speaking out against the severe and widespread problem of antisemitism. Most importantly, Labour Students, who have been allies of the Union of Jewish Students for decades, and today is no different. These people are the true anti-racists.

The Jewish community stands united in opposition to antisemitism. It does not stand in opposition to one political leader, or one political

party. Like so many others in my community, I do not leave the Labour Party because my politics or values have changed, rather because the Party has made clear through its actions that I am not welcome. Words mean nothing when the actions of so many speak louder.
I will continue to fight for a just and equal society, where racism is challenged and no citizen is left behind. However, I now know that the Labour Party is not the place where this battle is fought. My Jewish values led me to join the Labour Party, and now my being Jewish leaves me no choice but to resign.

Hannah Rose

26th October 2018
Colin Appleby
Cities of London and Westminster CLP Exec
JLM Delegate

To: Jennie Formby, General Secretary Labour Party

Dear Mrs. Formby,
I am dismayed at what the Labour Party has become in recent years. We have gone from being a party that could occupy the moral high ground to one that is rotten to the core.
Hatred and intolerance should have no place in a modern political movement and yet they have been welcomed in by our current leadership. They've been nurtured and have taken root and are now endemic at every level within Labour.
Jeremy Corbyn pays lip service to dealing with antisemitism. If anyone suggests that he's in any way responsible for the growth of antisemitism within the party he replies by saying that he's against all forms of racism and that he's campaigned against it for years. But words are not enough.
Over time, as you might be able to perceive, I've grown disenchanted with both Corbyn and the Corbyn Project. He claims to be on the "right side of history" but he is not.
When Russian agents poisoned people in Salisbury he said we needed to have more proof

before responding. When Hamas encourages Palestinians to storm the border fence between Gaza and Israel he calls for arms sales to Israel to stop. He says we shouldn't interfere in decisions taken by other sovereign nations. His message is inconsistent. He says we should defend human rights and fight for the oppressed, yet he stood in Parliament and made an impassioned speech for the UK not to intervene to save the Yazidis. He was against intervention in Kosovo. He's said nothing about the treatment meted out to Muslims or Christians by China. He always wants to intervene in Israel however.

If he'd ever apologised for holding Israel to a higher standard than any other country, then I'd think differently of the man but he hasn't. He is taking us all for fools.

I was a delegate at Conference in Liverpool. It wasn't a welcoming place for a Jew.

At breakfast on Monday, I was joined by two people I'd not met before. They hadn't met each other before. They were both delegates. The ease with which they segued from talking about breakfast to agreeing that Jews were "subhuman", "didn't deserve to be allowed to define what constitutes antisemitism" and should "be grateful we don't make them eat bacon for breakfast every day" stunned me. To my eternal shame I said nothing and left the table.

Many will say it's not antisemitic to criticise the Israeli government and no it isn't. The Israeli government under Netanyahu is a right-wing government that I do not support. That I've been asked in meetings to state whether or not I'm a fan of his government is antisemitic. That I've been asked this question, or a variant thereof many times, is shocking. What's more shocking still is that I've been told "shut up Jew" when I've voiced an unpopular opinion.

At Conference I was fearful of the hatred that the Palestine debate would unleash. I heard cries of "Free Free Palestine" and "From the river to the sea", a call for nothing less than the eradication of Israel, the only Jewish homeland in the world.

I voted against the Palestine motion because it was a poorly worded motion. I was one of about 15 who voted against. Delegates sitting behind me called me "child killer" and hissed at me. Not a hiss like you'd hear whilst watching a pantomime but a quiet persistent hiss like the sound gas makes when it's escaping from a pipe.

On Wednesday I sat with another delegate I'd not met before. They were firmly of the opinion that Corbyn was being held back from power by "the rich bankers and Jews that control the media". They told me of a huge conspiracy that was behind every war, funded ISIS, owned the Bank of England and the Federal Reserve, created HIV, caused the downfall of communism and was responsible for the slave trade. This conspiracy was so huge that it reached into every facet of our lives. This conspiracy had a name and it was

Zionism. I told them that I was Jewish and they asked “yes but are you a Zionist?”
I do not accept that those at the core of the Corbyn Project have unknowingly allowed the party to be tainted by antisemitism. I think it’s a deliberate tactic. They encourage JVL, who were established for one reason only and that’s to protect Corbyn. They are are crying out for a seat at the table and it seems to me that they want to remove JLM from their position as the official representatives of Jewish members.

I’ve fallen out of love with Labour.
I’ve been called a Zionazi.
I’ve been asked if I was a Zionist.
I’ve been called a Tory Jew.
I’ve been told I’m good with money.
I’ve been told that I’m “obviously” rich.
I’ve been accused of being more loyal to Israel than the U.K.
I’ve been called a child killer.
I’ve been barred from attending a JVL meeting.
I’ve been told “to shut the fuck up Jew”.
I’ve been screamed at in the street because I wanted JLM to address a local party meeting. I’ve been told I only ever care about Jewish stuff
I’ve been called Zio scum.
I’ve been told I’m worthless.
I’ve been told I’m a disgrace.
I’ve been told Hitler was right.
I’ve been told “it’s a pity all of your lot weren’t

gassed”.
I’ve been spat at.
I’ve been threatened with physical violence.
I’ve reported every single incident.
I’ve been told it’s all lies.
I’ve been told I’m part of a conspiracy to get Corbyn
I’ve been told I don’t belong in Labour.

They’re right about that, I’m a Jew and I don’t belong in Labour. I’m done.
I resign my membership.

Colin Appleby

20th December 2018
Ivan Lewis
Member of Parliament for Bury South 1997-2019

Rt Hon Jeremy Corbyn MP
Leader of the Opposition
House of Commons

Dear Jeremy,

It is with great sadness that I am writing to confirm my decision to resign from the Labour Party with immediate effect.

As you are aware, I have been suspended from the party for over twelve months, despite never having been interviewed about complaints which have been made against me. Emails the party were forced to make available to me show clearly the party could have moved forward with the disciplinary process from April but chose not to for political reasons.

This unnecessary and politically motivated delay occurred despite the fact that the party was fully aware of the impact the situation was having on my mental health.

In October when I made it clear to the party that I was considering resigning as I could no longer reconcile my Jewish identity and current Labour politics, a sudden attempt was made to move the process forward. This followed political control of the National Constitutional Committee passing to

your supporters. This is a process which is flawed and subject to political manipulation. I have made it clear that I strongly refute the charges which have been made and I am willing to cooperate with a truly independent process.
This is not the first time I have experienced a similar response to me raising concerns about antisemitism. I was the first former shadow cabinet minister you chose to sack when you became leader. You will recall sacking me by text message after I had asked to meet with you to discuss antisemitism.
It is for others to determine whether you are antisemitic, but what is absolutely clear is that you and Seamus Milne do not believe in the right of Jewish people to self-determination in their own state. This is different to your view on the right to self-determination for every other minority community. I believe in a negotiated two state solution; you should be honest and acknowledge your preference is that there should only be a state of Palestine. To compound this, all too often you have been unwilling to condemn those whose hatred of Israel becomes Jew hatred; this is incompatible with being a lifelong campaigner against racism.
This is integral to your anti-Western world view as you regard Israel as a proxy of the United States in the Middle East. Your long standing preferences are for the values of Putin's Russia and the Islamist fundamentalism of Iran.

It is no wonder that so many British people are uncomfortable at the prospect of you becoming Prime Minister of one of the world's most enduring western liberal democracies. On Brexit they sense your discomfort as a lifelong Eurosceptic seeking to conceal your true beliefs from your ardent supporters within the party who are overwhelmingly pro-European.

This drag on Labour's support is a blow most of all to those who are the victims of universal credit, the lack of any national child poverty strategy and the dismantling of so many frontline public services. The people who most need a Labour Government.

Nothing you say or do can change my sense of pride at being part of the Blair and Brown Governments which changed this country so much for the better. I'm proud to have made a contribution working with others to rebuild a modern apprenticeship system, introduce the dignity of personalisation to social care services and ensure maternal health became a global development priority.

My great sense of pride at representing the community where I was born and raised has never diminished. I'm humbled to have been elected on six successive occasions in a former Conservative seat. The support and loyalty shown to me by so many local people of all political persuasions especially during the past year has been truly moving.

As MP for Bury South I will continue to fight for local people on issues such as town centre regeneration, a new secondary school and improved mental health services. I will always owe a great debt of gratitude to the activists and my many friends in Bury South Labour Party who have worked so hard with me over the past twenty eight years to make our community a better place. I know we will always have a special bond which transcends the national party.

Ivan Lewis MP

13th February 2019
Councillor Dany Louise
Old Hastings Ward
Hastings Borough Council

To Peter Chowney
Council Leader, Hastings & Rye

13th February 2019

Dear Peter,

It is with regret and some relief that I am today resigning from the Labour Party.

Under Jeremy Corbyn and John McDonnell it has become a welcoming environment for antisemites. Despite numerous calls for the leadership to deal with antisemitism in the Party effectively, unequivocally, and speedily, they have failed to do so over a period of several years. Antisemitism remains not just tolerated within the party, but it eems, actively encouraged.

The day before Holocaust Memorial Day three Labour Party officials were welcomed back into the Party despite their antisemitic views and comments. This has happened too many times, and does not give confidence that there is a robust system in place, or the sincere will to properly address the huge rise of antisemitism amongst the Party membership.

The treatment of Luciana Berger MP has been disgraceful. She was faced with a vote of no confidence in her CLP. This action was met with a call for her to prove her loyalty to the Party by John McDonnell, and deafening silence by Jeremy Corbyn. Luciana Berger is an inspiring role-model, and a real-life contemporary hero. She should be celebrated as a person and MP of outstanding courage and integrity. It is unacceptable that Jeremy Corbyn and John McDonell were prepared to throw her to the wolves they have encouraged into the Party.

The treatment by the party of Dame Margaret Hodge MP was equally disgraceful. The continued abuse of John Mann MP, Rachel Riley and many others of lower profile by vile antisemitic "JC4PM" activists is another national scandal.

The level of denial by Jeremy Corbyn supporters leaves me in despair. Decent people hold their hands up in horror when the victims tell them they are being antisemitic. People and institutions who are sincere about not being racist learn to change their attitudes, behaviour and procedures for the better. They recognise that they have rightly been called out for unacceptable behaviour. It should be a cause for national concern that so many Labour Party members swear blind that antisemitism is "a smear against the leadership" despite the thousands of pieces of evidence in the public domain that Labour supporters behave in antisemitic ways. This

implies that their own and others' behaviour and attitudes are acceptable, which they are not.
It also feels extremely dangerous. This is the sort of self-righteous dogmatism, ignorance, and denial of facts that enabled the Holocaust.

The NCC has appointees on it who are themselves accused of antisemitism. There is no transparency about how cases are dealt with and many unanswered questions regarding the number of cases and the criteria used to judge them. This and the culture encouraged by the leadership makes the Labour Party institutionally antisemitic, in my own and others' opinion. As such, I can no longer be associated with it.
I have struggled with all this for many months and concluded that doing nothing implicates me. I am not willing to turn a blind eye to this situation. While this leadership remains, I cannot campaign for Labour in the next general election. I believe they are unfit for high-office: because of their handling of this issue, because of their inability to provide a credible opposition at a time when the Tories are disintegrating, and because of their problematic foreign policy.
Neither can I vote for an antisemitic government. I won't vote Conservative and I am therefore disenfranchised along with many thousands of other people. This is an appalling situation which greatly saddens me. I am a lifelong Labour voter who believes that universal suffrage is the first

and last line of defence between citizenry and dictatorship.
Apparently 6000 people a month are resigning their Labour Party membership. I am both saddened and relieved to be in their company.
I put myself forward as a councillor because I wanted to give something back to the town that has given me so much. I will continue to represent the needs of Old Hastings residents to the best of my ability until my term finishes in May 2020.
Enough really is Enough

Councillor Dany Louise

18th February 2019
Luciana Berger
Member of Parliament for Liverpool Wavertree 2010-2019

Dear Constituent,

I have today resigned from the Labour Party. This has been a very difficult, painful but necessary decision.

I have come to the conclusion having seen and experienced the Labour leadership first -hand and the direction the party has taken. I cannot, in good conscience, campaign for Jeremy Corbyn to become Prime Minister.

I have been a member of the Labour Party and have campaigned for it all my political life. The Labour values and traditions I grew up with, that run deep through my family history, have not changed. The core value of equality – for all – opportunity – for all – anti-racism – against all – and social justice – the values which I hold really dear and which led me to join the Labour Party as a student almost 20 years ago, remain who I am. Devastatingly and in sharp contrast, the Labour Party, its culture and what it stands for has become wholly unrecognisable.

The leadership's disdain for internationalism and for our country's national security underline just how far removed the party is from the most fundamental Labour beliefs. The lack of leadership to stand up and challenge the blindfold

Brexit our country is stumbling towards, enables the savage consequences it will have on the employment opportunities and prosperity for our constituency.

The reality is that the party is being driven by an unconditional commitment to a failed, inward-looking and dangerous ideology of the past. We were promised an era of "kinder, gentler politics" and yet the ideological hard left which now runs the party has embedded a culture of bullying, closedmindedness and bigotry towards anyone with differing views. All while nothing has been done in response, except to stand by and wilfully watch.

As a proud member of the British Jewish community, I have also seen the Labour Party allow antisemitism to take root and fester in a way that is unprecedented in modern British politics. We were told that zero tolerance would be extended to antisemites in Labour's ranks, and yet in reality the situation has only got worse.

It was nearly a year ago that we saw the unprecedented event of a minority community, the Jewish community, take to Parliament Square to demonstrate against the Labour Party and say Enough is Enough. And yet since then, despite a mountain of evidence, we have only seen the situation of racism against Jewish people within its ranks worsen.

I believe there is an undeniable chasm between the values held by those at the helm of the

Labour Party and those of my constituents and the country. I cannot now see a way to bring the Labour Party back to its historic focus on community, tolerance, fairness and respect – values to which I am wholly committed.

I will continue to give my all to the people of Liverpool Wavertree. I am proud of what we have achieved together, since I was first elected to represent you nine years ago. I will continue to stand up for our local NHS, in particular our mental health services; the right of every child to have the best start in life; and for those who pay the price of inequality in our community.

There is much more to be done and my focus and effort will remain working alongside, and for you my constituents, to secure a better and fairer future for all.

Luciana Berger MP

18th February 2019
Mike Gapes
Member of Parliament Ilford South 1992-2019

Dear Constituents

I am writing to you today to inform you that I have, this morning resigned from the Labour Party.

This has not been an easy or sudden decision. I joined the Labour Party fifty years ago aged 16. I have been active at all levels, from Redbridge Young Socialist Branch Treasurer, to Chair of the National Organisation of Labour Students. I worked for fifteen years at Labour Party Head Office including as head of the International Section. Since 1992 I have been your Labour and Co-operative Member of Parliament for Ilford South.

I have always considered myself Labour to my core. I have many good friends in the Labour Party locally, nationally and internationally. I care passionately about traditional Labour values of fairness, social justice, equality and internationalism. I will never put the national security of our country at risk. I will fight for strong UK defence and security inside NATO and to remain in the EU. I will continue to support the global rules based system which our country helped to establish and which is now under threat from Trump and Putin.

Recent political positions taken by the leadership of the Labour Party have been increasingly difficult to justify or support. This is not the Labour Party I joined or have supported for so many years.

I am sickened that Labour is now perceived by many as a racist, antisemitic party. The National Executive Committee did eventually, despite the opposition of the Party Leader, agree to the full International Holocaust Remembrance Alliance definition of antisemitism and all working examples. But there has been considerable reluctance since then to seriously deal with hundreds of cases of antisemitism and several prominent antisemites have been readmitted to the Party.

It is increasingly clear that prominent figures in the Corbyn Labour leadership do not want to stop Brexit. Indeed they are now complicit in facilitating Brexit, which will cause great economic, social and political damage to our country. They whipped Labour MPs to trigger Article 50. They opposed amendments which would have kept the UK in the Single Market and European Economic Area. They have delayed and obstructed attempts to implement the agreed policy of the 2018 Labour Party Conference to secure a People's Vote with the option to Remain in the EU.

Jeremy Corbyn and those around him, are also on the wrong side on so many international issues

from Russia, to Syria, to Venezuela. If he ever became Prime Minister it would be a threat to our national security and international alliances.
I have always worked hard to represent the interests of my constituents and my country. I must be true to myself and my values. I must also be honest with my constituents. A Corbyn government would threaten the prosperity and security of our country. I cannot support that. I am therefore resigning from the Labour Party.
Members of Parliament are not party delegates. They are the elected representatives of their constituents. I am pleased that my constituents have elected me seven times, and that my majority has increased from 402 in 1992 to 31,647 in 2017.
It has been a great privilege and honour to represent my constituents for 27 years; to serve my diverse, vibrant, growing constituency; to fight for Crossrail; to fight to save King George Hospital; and to be part of the Labour government team that negotiated the Northern Ireland Good Friday Agreement.
My office has helped tens of thousands of constituents on issues like housing, health, education, benefits, transport, asylum and immigration. We will continue to do so. I will continue to be your local man, with a national and international voice. I will now represent you in Parliament as a member of the new Independent Group of MPs.

If you have any issues to raise on any matter please do not hesitate to contact me.

Mike Gapes MP

18th February 2019
Joe Goldberg
Labour Cabinet Member and Councillor, London Borough of Haringey
Candidate in Witney against David Cameron 2010

Jennie Formby
General Secretary, The Labour Party

Dear Jennie,
In 2015 I wrote an opinion piece for Jewish News, where I made clear that unless action was taken on the ambivalence towards antisemitism, it would take hold within the party. Nearly four years later, I am saddened to see little action has been taken, and that the virus has indeed taken hold in ways I thought unimaginable for a party whose core beliefs centre on equality, tolerance and respect.
I have been a party member for over 23 years. I joined because I had known nothing but a Tory government and the indignity of poverty it had served up to people across the country. I was desperate to help bring Labour to power to deliver a more socially and economically just society. To be clear I believe the last Labour government did just that.
My love and dedication to the Party runs deep. I have knocked on thousands of doors, attended hundreds of meetings. I took the fight to David Cameron in his own back yard as a Labour PPC,

fought and won an extremely tough by-election in Haringey, served as a Councillor for nearly ten years, and currently sit on the London Regional Board.

We named our son, Keir, not just because of the role Keir Hardie played in the Labour Party, but because, in spite of some unsavoury attitudes about Jews, he was one of the first to recognize the need to take up the cause of Jewish refugees in London.

There is a poignant moment in the film, Three Billboards Outside Ebbing, Missouri, where Fargo turns to the priest and says "Because you joined the gang, man. And I don't care if you never did sh*t or never saw sh*t, or never heard sh*t. You joined the gang. You're culpable."

I and many Jewish members have seen and heard too much for too long. It is clear to me that the party is either wilfully or otherwise unable to contain this virus. Too many individuals from the NEC and the Leader's office down have given permission for people to speak and act in ways that are simply vile. The lack of action is nothing short of a signal of consent for behaviour such as Jackie Walker's that stand in contradiction to the spirit and the letter of our party's long held values of equality and antiracism. The tolerance of people like Chris Williamson is just a case in point, as are the sympathies expressed by John McDonnell.

In my own case I have seen Nazi materials posted

on CLP Facebook forums being upheld as acceptable behaviour, have seen the Leader of my borough be allowed to talk about "antisemitism being weaponized" – denying and undermining Jewish people the right to identify moments of discrimination against them. I have seen "comrade" Councillors excused the whip on a motion against antisemitism on the basis of "conscientious objection." I have seen countless articulation of tropes that are antisemitic spouted in meetings, I have seen Jenny Rathbone let back into the Welsh Assembly group after just six weeks with very little to show for it and no apparent action by the Party, and I have even had a local Member of Parliament threaten me with legal action – three times - after I spoke of my experiences on World At One. This is not the actions of a party getting to grips with antisemitism.

The bullying and intimidation of Luciana Berger have been disgusting, and I stand in absolute solidarity for her courage and conviction. It is why I can no longer remain a "part of the gang" when senior people in the Labour movement use my own continued membership as a legitimacy for their own.

It is why I am writing to you today to resign my membership from the Labour Party.

We used to be a party of principles, of values. We didn't win in 1997 because we were calculated. We won because we had conviction. The

leadership were able to put forward their promise on a record they could stand behind.
Today we are led by people who cannot take responsibility for their past actions or words and won't take action on the current crisis of antisemitism. Fundamentally, I want to ensure that when I look my son and daughter in the eyes, that I am not culpable for the danger to their future that Corbyn, yourself and the rest of the Labour Party present to them. Those that now choose to remain a part of the gang sadly are.

Joe Goldberg

18th February 2019
Adam Langleben
Former Labour Councillor for West Hendon,
London Borough of Barnet
Chipping Barnet CLP
Jewish Labour Movement National Executive Committee

Dear Jeremy Corbyn,

I joined the Labour Party 13 years ago as a student on the left of the party, a place I have remained throughout my time in Labour — supporting the trade union movement, the 'soft left' and voting for Ed Miliband to become Leader — a decision I now greatly regret.

My reason for becoming a Labour supporter, member and later an elected Councillor was my complete assurance of the shared values of the Labour Party and my own Jewish faith, community and heritage. A complete and utter commitment to anti-racism, social justice and the eradication of economic injustice. It has now become clear that under your leadership, the party has been corrupted and indoctrinated by people who are authoritarian in their approach to politics, encourage democratic structures that lead to bullying mob rule, and above all else — are racist towards Jews — which may well be a result of the approach of the two latter philosophies. History is clear to me that when political events like this begin with Jews, they never end with Jews. All minorities should, and I believe will eventually have significant reason to worry about your rise to the leadership of the Labour Party.

There can be no racial, social or economic justice whilst antisemites have completed a hostile takeover of the greatest force for achieving those aims. Antisemitism is a corrosive conspiracy theory that blocks the achievement of all justices. You represent the ultimate betrayal of Labour values. I thought naively that it and you could be changed. That very naivety or belief in the good in people is why I and so many others are part of the Labour Party. You have abused and manipulated the idealism of hundreds of thousands of good people, whilst allowing the antisemites to become evangelists for hate.

Too many people I have known for my whole life are now asking themselves for the very first time if they have a future in this country if you win power. Questions unimaginable for Jewish people just five years ago. People who are committed to the same values that the Labour Party once stood for. I cannot be part of helping you rise to become Prime Minister.

Mr Corbyn, you must take full responsibility for this. Prior to your leadership of this once great party antisemitism was minimal — during your tenure antisemites have roamed free, have spread their venom to people who previously had no experience, knowledge or feelings towards Jews and this poison has turned ordinary people who genuinely believe themselves to be anti-racists into bigots — all whilst you buried your own head in the sand because of a complete emotional inability to comprehend the harsh reality that you yourself have been surrounded by antisemites for decades and perhaps are an antisemite.

You, Seumas Milne, Karie Murphy, Len McClusky, the bullies at the top have all allowed this culture of institutionalised antisemitism to develop and grow. You have fed a culture of denial that has allow this sickness to spread. You brief Alt-Left media such as Skwawkbox, which disseminates your message to distrust Jews en masse.

I believe this is an institutional problem of antisemitism that cannot be eradicated on your watch. Some good people who are fellow travellers of yours do understand the issue but are powerless to do anything about it. Some of your own advisors have told me that they believe you to be an antisemite but want to try and change you. But you cannot be changed.

Out of respect for them I will not name them. However, whilst they may be able to live with this knowledge, I cannot.

Over the past year I have had too many conversations with people in and around your office and the leadership of the broad left who I believe genuinely wish to eradicate antisemitism within our party but are fearful of raising their concerns too loudly within your office out of fear of retribution, demotion or simply being locked out of a tight knit clique of those now running the Labour Party. This is why the problem is institutional, even the people who want to fix it are powerless to because of those at the top. A top team managed by you, perhaps even under instruction by you.

Our Party has become institutionally racist on your watch in just four short years. Every complaint I have submitted about antisemitism in our party remains outstanding. Laura Stuart, Jackie Walker, Steve Walker and a dossier of 250 people that JLM submitted, amongst too many others to name.

Many of the people who stay, including those in Momentum, I have the upmost respect for and they will come to their own conclusions in their own time. But I can have no further part in this. My wife and I are having our first child in two weeks time. One day my son may ask me what I did to stop you from ever becoming Prime Minister. I can no longer look my family and friends in the face without complete shame.

Well this is something small, but I will no longer be part of this. I will no longer pay subscriptions to an antisemitic movement. I will sign one pledge and that is to stop a party led by antisemites from ever gaining power in this country and I will continue to live by the values on the back of my now torn up membership card.

Please consider this my resignation from the Labour Party.

Adam Langleben

19th February 2019
Joan Ryan
Member of Parliament Enfield North 1997-2010 and 2015-2019

Statement on the Labour Party

After four decades, I have made the terribly difficult decision that I can no longer remain a member of the Labour Party and have today resigned from it.
It has been an enormous honour and privilege to serve as a Labour councillor, MP and minister over the past 25 years and I never believed I would be forced to leave the party.
I am hugely grateful for the chance to serve. None of this would have been possible without Labour Party members who have campaigned with and for me.
But the values that led me to join the Labour Party are the same values that have led me to leave it today.
My mum and dad both came from Ireland. Their working lives were hard: they had manual jobs and often faced discrimination, but they wanted – and achieved – something different and better for their children. Good schools and my parents' hard work gave my sisters and I a great start in life, a university education and decent jobs.

I learned from my mum and dad the dignity of work and the evil of racism and prejudice. I also learned the value of solidarity. I saw how, through the Irish Club my dad was the secretary of, people stuck together, helped each other through the hard times, and treated each other with fairness and decency.

That experience and those values led me to join the Labour Party. Equality is the Labour Party's founding principle: providing a better, fairer future for all our children and grandchildren.

That requires and demands that we stand up to racism in all its forms; a principle which all previous Labour leaders and the Labour governments of Harold Wilson, Jim Callaghan, Tony Blair and Gordon Brown upheld and honoured.

Over the past three years, however, the Labour Party under Jeremy Corbyn has become infected with the scourge of anti-Jewish racism. This problem simply did not exist in the party before his election as leader. No previous Labour leader would have allowed this huge shame to befall the party.

I have always believed that we must be especially vigilant against the oldest hatred; history teaches us the tragic and horrific results of a failure to do so.

I have been horrified, appalled and angered to see the Labour leadership's dereliction of duty in the face of this evil.

Over the past year, I have visited synagogues, attended demonstrations against antisemitism and spoken to Jewish constituents on doorsteps. On every occasion, I have seen and heard bewilderment, fear and anger. At all times, I pledged my solidarity and promised action.

Today, having fought for as long as I can within the Labour Party, I honour my pledge of solidarity.

I cannot remain a member of the Labour Party while its leadership allows Jews to be abused with impunity and the victims of such abuse to be ridiculed, have their motives questioned, and their integrity called into doubt.

I cannot remain a member of the Labour Party while its leadership singles out for demonization and delegitimization the world's only Jewish state.

And I cannot remain a member of the Labour Party while this requires me to suggest that I believe Jeremy Corbyn – a man who has presided over the culture of anti-Jewish racism and hatred for Israel which now afflicts my former party – is fit to be Prime Minister of this country. He is not.

The Labour leadership has pledged action against antisemitism for three years. At every turn, it has resisted, ignored and snubbed the legitimate demands of the Jewish community, made through their representative institutions.

Instead, it has offered white-wash reports.

It has operated a revolving door disciplinary policy with those accused of antisemitism briefly suspended and then quietly readmitted to the party.

And it has allowed its surrogates to belittle the scale of the problem and attack those who try to bring it to light.

Last summer, after Labour's behaviour had forced Jews to demonstrate in Parliament Square; after the party had refused to adopt in full the International Holocaust Remembrance Alliance definition of antisemitism; and after weeks of revelations about his own alleged links to Holocaust deniers, antisemites and terrorists, Jeremy Corbyn had but one priority: to preserve the right of antisemites to label Israel a "racist endeavour".

That priority tells me all I need to know about his fitness to lead the Labour Party and our country.

There is only one credible explanation for such behaviour.

It is that anti-Jewish racism and the sensitivities of British Jews simply do not matter enough to the Labour leadership.

Given a choice between the support of antisemites, and ridding the party of Jew-hate, they have decided to side with the antisemites.

I refuse to accept that choice and I wish to stand with British Jews and Jewish members of the Labour Party and Members of Parliament who have suffered terrible abuse from supporters of the Labour leadership.

I salute Luciana Berger on her courageous stand against antisemitism. I pay tribute as well to those, such as the wonderful Dame Louise Ellman, who have decided to continue the fight from within the Labour Party. I wish them, and stalwart allies such as Tom Watson, only the very best in their continuing efforts and I hope my decision will help the much-needed process of real action and change.

But for now, anti-Jewish racism, we are told, cannot be eradicated within the party and it would be "foolish" to pretend otherwise.

I cannot in good conscience support or represent a party which adopts such an attitude. The British people deserve so much better.

The antisemitism crisis has thrown a harsh light on the values and behaviour of Jeremy Corbyn's Labour Party.

Like its populist ideological bedfellows, it evinces a disdain for the rights of minorities, and adopts a bullying, aggressive attitude to those who dare to question its cult-like received wisdom.

It engages in bizarre, offensive and dangerous conspiracy theories – ones often founded on classic antisemitic tropes evoking the powerful hidden hand of "Rothschilds", Zionists and the

"Israel lobby" – and sets aside the truth when politically inconvenient.

And it has replaced Labour's traditional message of openness, hope and optimism with an all-consuming narrative founded on rage, betrayal and the hunt for heretics.

I do not believe that such an attitude – one that is all too reminiscent of Donald Trump's Republican party, the European far right and some, but by no means all, Brexiteers – is in the least bit healthy for society or for our democracy.

The first duty of any government is the safety and security of its citizens.

The Jewish community has made clear that it believes a Jeremy Corbyn government would be an existential threat to it. I will not campaign to put such a government into office.

If the threat a Corbyn government posed were simply to Jews,that would be reason enough for me to do all that I can to oppose such a threat.

But it is an oft-state truism that what starts with Jews never ends with Jews.

The mindset, ideology and worldview that tolerates antisemitism poses a threat to the British public, Jew and non-Jew alike.

It is one that would rip up the alliances which have kept our country safe for the past seven decades.

It is one that would ostracise the Middle East's only democracy in favour of the Ayatollahs in Tehran: a regime which tramples on human rights, has the blood of tens of thousands of Syrians on its hands, and seeks to dominate and subjugate the region and impose its theocratic brutal rule.

And it is one that would abandon our friends in Europe in favour of appeasing Vladimir Putin: the head of a country which launched a chemical weapons attack on British soil, but which – despite a mountain of evidence and the conclusions of the intelligence community – Jeremy Corbyn repeatedly refused to blame the Russian state for.

Nine years of Tory government have caused enormous damage to my constituency and the country.

Held hostage by the hard right of her party, the Prime Minister is now preparing to inflict a crippling hard Brexit – one that will rob the young of their future.

Jeremy Corbyn and the Stalinist clique that surrounds him offers no real opposition to any of this, instead they are too busy purging their perceived ideological enemies within and obsessing over issues that are of little interest to the British people.

I will continue to fight for the values that the Labour Party has traditionally upheld – for equality, the eradication of poverty and discrimination, and a fair shot at their dreams for all our children and young people.

But I cannot and will not do that from within an institutionally antisemitic party.

Joan Ryan MP

21st February 2019
Dr David Hirsh,
Senior Lecturer Goldsmiths, University of London
Author of Complete Left Antisemitism

This is my resignation from the Labour Party, my political home since I was 18 years old.
Personally, I have had enough of being humiliated by antisemitism in the Labour movement. I have fought it for years, in the student movement in the academic unions and in the Labour Party. I won't subject myself to it any longer.
Politically, the most important thing to me at the moment is democracy. I mean by that our democratic states in which we look after each other and our civil society in which we are free to do what we choose.
I mean the principle that human beings are in a fundamental sense of equal value, and so opposition to discrimination against people on the basis of their designated race, gender, sexuality, religion or nation is a fundamental principle.
I mean a free economy, within a legal framework which nurtures creativity, vibrancy and efficiency and which also which sets out terrains in which enterprises agree not to compete: like health and safety, holiday pay, maternity leave, equality and workers' rights. A democratically calibrated and constrained free economy is the most successful way of combating inequality.

I mean international trade, cosmopolitan institutions and universal friendship; I mean democracy and democratic rights and values across the world; and solidarity with those fighting for them.

I mean a high quality and efficient National Health Service; I mean excellent education available to all; and I mean a safety net which looks after people when they are unable to look after themselves.

I mean freedom of speech, freedom of religion, freedom of association and free trade unions.

I mean the democratic right to pursue happiness and to make one's own relationships and networks.

Antisemitism threatens Jews but it is also always an indicator of the ascendancy of an anti-democratic political culture in any community in which it is tolerated.

I am afraid of the rise of populist politics which I understand as a set of radical threats to democracy as described above. Populist movements try to harness the politics of fury and resentment for the political advancement of those who assume the right to speak for 'the people' and to treat those they don't like as 'enemies of the people'.

Populism replaces debate and respect for knowledge with an essentialism which designates people as enemies not because of what they say or do but because of who they are.

The Corbyn movement, which is well entrenched in the Labour Party, is such a movement. The Brexit movement which is well entrenched in the Tory Party, and in the Corbyn faction too, is also a populist movement. Both Labour and the Tories are trying to ride the tiger of populism and are prepared to risk British democracy and prosperity to do so. The tiger will maul them and it will maul us all in the end.

Jihadi Islamism and other fundamentalisms are also radical critiques of democracy of a related kind.

Populism sees nothing of value in existing society and it promises to tear everything down and to begin again from zero; experience shows that it is easier to destroy than to create.

I want to be part of a movement which defends democratic principles, as outlined above, and which defends us against the populist threats, also as outlined above.

This is not a conservative manifesto. There is nowhere near enough democracy in our world. The defence and creation of democratic states and movements is a programme for radical change; and for radical change in what people are enthusiastic about. And it is urgent.

There are many other issues which people take seriously and with justification; the threat of climate change for example. Addressing these requires democracy. Without that, we're finished.

But within that framework we can decide, together, what needs to be done.
I do not want Jeremy Corbyn to be the next Prime Minister; he is so wedded to antisemitic politics that he has been quite unable to address the antisemitic culture which he imported into the Labour mainstream. And that is linked to his anti-democratic worldview. While Corbyn himself may not be around for very long as leader, his politics and his culture will be, in my judgement.
Some have argued that if democratic people, not least democratic Jews, leave the Labour Party then this will allow free reign to those who embrace antisemitic and proto-totalitarian politics.
Yes, if we leave, that is what will happen. But it happens when we don't leave too. So now people who consider themselves socialists will have to take responsibility for the culture in their own movement. Because I'm done. And I think most other Jews are done too.

Dr David Hirsh

22nd February 2019
Ian Austin
Member of Parliament Dudley North 2005-2019

Letter to constituents

Dear XXX
I have taken the difficult decision to leave the Labour Party and the first thing I wanted to do was to write to you straight away and tell you why.
I grew up in Dudley and love the place. Being the local MP is the greatest privilege in the world and I am so grateful to have the chance to serve this community. I work hard every day to repay the confidence people have placed in me and I promise I will carry on working just as hard to help local people, stand up for Dudley and improve things in the area.
I learnt important values growing up in Dudley. The importance of fairness and playing by the rules. Knowing what's right and what's wrong. Basic decent British values.
I grew up listening to my Dad – a refugee from the Holocaust – teaching me about the evils of hatred and prejudice. One of the main reasons I joined the Labour Party as a teenager here in Dudley more than 35 years ago was to fight racism, and I could never have believed that I'd be leaving because of racism too.

I have fought intolerance and prejudice all my life. Our first campaign when I became an MP was to work with local councillors and community groups to drive the BNP out of Dudley. Last year I organised a Rally Against Racism in the Birmingham hotel where Enoch Powell made his "Rivers of Blood" speech 50 years before. I've stood with Muslim constituents targeted by the BNP or the EDL and I will always fight for a more tolerant and united society.

The Labour Party has been my life, so this has been the hardest decision I have ever had to take, but I have to be honest and the truth is that I have become ashamed of the Labour Party under Jeremy Corbyn.

I am appalled at the offence and distress Jeremy Corbyn and the Labour Party have caused to Jewish people.

It is terrible that a culture of extremism, antisemitism and intolerance is driving out good MPs and decent people who have committed their life to mainstream politics.

It is wrong that Luciana Berger has been bullied out of the Labour Party by antisemites. It is wrong that the party threatened Margaret Hodge when she spoke out on antisemitism, like they threatened me when I raised the issue with the party chairman. They had to back down because we had done nothing wrong, but the hard truth is that the party is tougher on the people

complaining about antisemitism than it is on the antisemites.
Jeremy Corbyn and the people around him have turned a mainstream party into something very different. He has spent his entire political career working with and supporting all sorts of extremists, and in some cases terrorists and antisemites. I always thought he was unfit to lead the Labour Party and I certainly think he is unfit to lead our country.
I think Jeremy Corbyn and John McDonnell cannot be trusted with our national security and would undermine our democratic institutions.
They supported the IRA when they were planting bombs and murdering people in shopping centres, hotels and pubs. They back totalitarian dictatorships like Venezuela abroad and echoed the Kremlin when Putin tried to murder people here in Britain.
I respect people in Dudley. I always tell them the truth and I could never ask local people to make him Prime Minister. That is why I have decided to leave the Labour Party.
Other decent MPs, councillors and members – good friends of mine – have chosen to remain. I know they share my concerns and it is not for me to call on them to leave, but I wish them well in their fight to improve things inside the party.
I will be an independent MP but I will be working just as hard to stand up for our area. Dudley has been hit hard by a decade of cutbacks. It is a

disgrace to see homeless people sleeping rough in the town centre. We have fewer police and rising levels of crime. People wait too long for GP appointments or hospital treatment. Many families are struggling to make ends meet. I'll work as hard as I always have to fight for our area and local people.

I will always do everything I can to help. My office in Trinity Road will be open as usual and I meet people in Dudley every week, either visiting them at home, at my office.

My priority is to work for people in Dudley. I'll be out and about knocking on doors to listen to residents just as usual, so let me know if you would like to join the team of local people who help support my campaigns.

Ian Austin MP

22nd February 2019
Former Councillor Warren Morgan
Former leader Brighton and Hove City Council

Dear Ms Formby,
I joined the Labour Party in 1993, having been persuaded by a friend at university, Tom Watson, that the party had changed and offered hope for the future. Like many, I was inspired by John Smith's words "the opportunity to serve our country; that is all we ask".
Ten years on I committed myself full time to the party, working for the local MP and being elected as a councillor to represent one of the most deprived wards in the South East. It has been an honour to serve the party and the residents of East Brighton for the past sixteen years, and it was a privilege to serve my city as council leader for three years until last May. Brighton and Hove was one of only two new Labour council administrations in 2015, something the party rewarded at Conference in the city that September.
As Leader I delivered more new council homes than at any time in three decades, and worked to ensure that despite massive Conservative cuts, no council staff faced compulsory redundancy. My excellent, talented, committed Labour council colleagues delivered dozens of achievements in the most challenging of circumstances. Yet more than half of those elected in 2015, when we went

from third place on 13 councillors to the largest group on 23, will not be on the ballot paper this May.

I was one of the first to raise concerns about antisemitism following events at the 2017 Conference in Brighton. It was my duty as council leader to call out racism wherever and whenever it appeared, without fear or favour, in defence of the city's Jewish community. For that I was vilified by members locally and supporters of Jeremy Corbyn nationally.

I won't detail the events in the local Labour Party prior to and since that time; suffice to say that many valued colleagues have been bullied out of the party, and some of those responsible remain suspended but not expelled. The absence of support for me and council colleagues by party staff has been extremely disappointing, the failure of the party to uphold its own values amongst its own members is unforgivable.

I am and always have been a European citizen with strong ties to France, and a passionate supporter of the European Union. Brighton and Hove voted overwhelmingly to remain in the EU, and it has appalled me that the leader of the party has in my view wilfully obfuscated and distorted his position in order to not comply with the intent of the policy set by members.

As for so many long-serving members and councillors, it has been made clear to me on many occasions by people who largely joined in

2015, often from other left wing parties, that I am no longer welcome. Indeed it has been argued I was never “real Labour" at all. It was made clear that I should stand down as council leader and would not win reselection.

Friends in the Jewish Labour Movement urged me not to resign my membership, as others have done, in response to the unchecked and rampant antisemitism amongst party members, in order to fight back and clear the party of those with racist antisemitic views. I have done so until now.

I came into politics to change society for the better, to win that opportunity to serve. I did not come into politics to spend all my time and energy fighting people in the same party. The racism, bullying and intolerance of any dissenting view is intolerable. It has ceased to be the broad church I joined.

I cannot remain a member of a party which supports and enables Brexit, which came about purely to win the Conservative Party the 2015 election, which was passed due to dog-whistle rhetoric on immigration, corrupt campaign practices, “dark ads" and online interference and decades of myths about the EU propagated by people who resented the restrictions the EU places on their business interests. Any form of Brexit will harm jobs, employment rights, pay and conditions, opportunities for young people, our NHS and our economic wellbeing. The people Labour represents, those who we give voice to, are the ones who will be harmed most. It is an act of utter betrayal and dogmatic ignorance by Jeremy Corbyn to support, and not oppose vigorously, this act of catastrophic national self-harm.

I despair at what the party I have devoted more than half my life to has become, and the far left doctrines and dogmas that now constrict it. I respect all those friends and colleagues who will stay as members, councillors and MPs, but it is with enormous sadness that I must now resign my membership of the Labour Party after 27 years. My values as a social democrat have not changed in that time and nor will they, but now like others I must find another means by which to realise those values, deliver better lives for the people who need representation, and give others that opportunity to serve.

Former councillor Warren Morgan

23rd February 2019
Former Councillor Rowan Draper

Dear Resident,
I write to inform you that I have resigned my membership of The Labour Party and resigned from the Labour Group of Councillors on Stafford Borough Council effective immediately.
Littleworth Councillor
The people of Littleworth have elected me twice under a Labour banner and I owe them my gratitude and my deepest thanks for the opportunity and their trust to serve them over the last eight years. As their advocate, I have argued for the protection of emergency services at Stafford Hospital, stood up for young people when the County Council slashed youth services and worked consistently on the Council to provide the rigorous scrutiny that any Council Leadership should welcome.
I want to take this time to highlight what I have been able to achieve as a member of Stafford Borough Council with support from my Labour Party colleagues:
In 2014 I gained recognition on a national shortlist of Young Councillors of the Year, through the Local Government Information Unit, because of my campaigning to support and defend our Hospital's emergency services.
In 2015 I was accepted onto the prestigious Next Generation scheme, organised by the Local

Government Association, which recognises and develops future leaders within Local Government. In 2016 I had the honour and privilege to serve the Borough as its second citizen, the youngest ever to do so on the authority, and the first Councillor from Littleworth ward to do so since the early 1990s.

In 2018 I was appointed to Labour's front bench on the Council, to serve as their Resources spokesperson, and elected cross-party to chair the Member Development Working Group.

The Labour Party and Antisemitism

Today, nearly a decade has passed since I took my first steps into political life and to my political home: The Labour Party. When I joined the party, as a passionate student, I had a desire to change the world, like many who have joined the party since the 2015 General Election defeat. Looking at my membership card today as I write this letter to you all I am struck by the words that have moved my action: "By the strength of our common endeavour we achieve more than we achieve alone .... We live together freely, in a spirit of solidarity, tolerance and respect."

Respect, Tolerance and Solidarity are anathema in today's Labour Party.

The election of Jeremy Corbyn as Leader of the Labour Party, along with the transformation of the party, has meant that the party has descended into the sewer. It is now a safe-haven for antisemites. Jeremy himself has failed to answer the calls of the Board of Deputies of British Jews and the Jewish Leadership Council, to allay the concerns and fears of the Jewish community, and to protect the party from becoming institutionally antisemitic. I feel his inaction shows his deep-seated desire to pit oppressor versus oppressed. His out-dated world view is not fit for our modern politics.

Attending heated party meetings where bullying is rife, along with sexism and intolerance, has been my experience of The Labour Party for a number of years even before Jeremy Corbyn. Sitting in rooms with people who do not share your values but want to humiliate and attack you at every turn will be no reasonable person's preferred course to be involved in politics. Labour's inability to deal effectively with bullying and intimidation within the party is a key factor in my decision today. If you can't protect your membership from racism and bullying, how do you expect to do so in Government?

Labour Leadership

Since the Labour Leadership Election campaign in 2015 my issues of conscience with Jeremy Corbyn has never been something I have shied away from, and I will not start now. I cannot and will not share an association with those who endorse terrorism, either in Ireland or in the Middle East. I have been emotionally torn over this decision and I do not make this lightly but I cannot in good conscience continue to allow my name to be associated with The Labour Party, or its Leader Jeremy Corbyn and the hard left machine around him.

I believe in a society that looks after each other, and that makes sure that people don't go without when they need help but I cannot place these values above my desire for a country that values its national security and does not leave us defenceless to those who would do us harm.

Friends and Colleagues

I am deeply upset that I will no longer share the party banner of so many friends and colleagues who I have had the privilege of knowing and campaigning with to deliver a fairer society. I hope that whilst I won't share the same rosette any longer I will continue to share the same Labour values that brought me into the party and serve as a Councillor for 8 years.

I want to place on record my sincerest gratitude to Aidan Godfrey, Labour's Leader on Stafford Borough Council, for the role he has played in my development on the Council. I thank him for the opportunity to serve our Party, our members and our voters as Resources Spokesperson on the Council.

Former Councillor Rowan Draper

24th February 2019
Group resignation letter from former Labour Councillors
Announced Sunday Times

Cllr Warren Morgan, Former Leader, Brighton & Hove City Council
Cllr Rowan Draper, Stafford Borough Council
Cllr Dany Louise, Hastings Borough Council
Cllr Frances Weetman, North Tyneside Council
Cllr John Ferrett, Portsmouth City Council
Ken Ferrett, former Councillor, Portsmouth City Council
Adam Langleben, former Councillor, London Borough of Barnet
James Patterson, former Councillor, London Borough of Haringey
And six others

Dear Sir,
We are Labour councillors and former Labour councillors. We have, after many years of dedicated membership, resigned from the Labour Party. We are writing to express our support for the former Labour MPs over their decision to resign and establish the Independent Group. Having witnessed up close the hard-left takeover of Labour, we believe that their harsh, uncompromising and dogmatic approach to politics poses a genuine threat.

In the last three years, we have seen hard-left campaigns destroy efforts by Labour councils to help our communities. Local authorities have faced impossible financial pressure and a growing demand for social care and housing. Many Labour councillors have been prepared to look beyond the state for solutions. All too often, this has resulted in them being subjected to fierce and dishonest campaigns from within the Labour Party membership. This leads us to believe a hard-left Labour government would severely harm the economy, threatening local services.
In the last three and a half years, the atmosphere within the Labour Party has changed beyond all recognition. A culture of bullying,intimidation and hostility towards Jewish people becoming common-place. Having seen this unfold locally we now believe Labour, in its current form, poses a direct threat, economically, socially, and culturally, should it ever come to power. Britain is facing huge challenges in the months and years ahead, not least due to Brexit. To have any chance of meeting those challenges, politics need to change. We therefore welcome the new Independent Group.

Richard Horton
Organiser/Secretary, Hillrise branch (2010-14)
Chair, Stroud Green branch (2017-18)

4th March 2019
To Jeremy Corbyn,

Dear Jeremy,
As we have known each other for over a decade and as I have knocked on thousands of residents' doors for you and with you in the various roles I had in Islington North CLP I thought I should write to you directly.
My politics has been formed by my life experience. Growing up in and around towns like Scunthorpe and Grimsby in the 1980s and 1990s, my student activism in the 2000s, being made redundant at the height of the global financial crisis and recently becoming a father have all shaped my values.
My first job after university was working for The Fabian Society. I voted for and actively campaigned for Ed Miliband in the 2010 leadership election. I was encouraged by our 2017 general election manifesto, which I found to be rooted in our social democratic traditions. Yes, I disagreed with some of the middle class freebies such as scrapping university tuition fees but I understood that you needed to build a coalition of support and drive enthusiasm among younger people to win. I even subscribed to *Tribune*

before it became fashionable. Some people in the Labour movement may go as far as calling me "soft left".

The mission to improve and equalise life chances defined my values when I joined the party and it still defines my values now. However, I no longer believe that Labour as an institution – the leadership, activists and apparatus – shares my values. The party's constitution remains social democratic but its culture is not. When I look at my membership card and read the quote from Clause IV printed on the reverse I cannot help but think there is a mile-wide gap between those ideals – solidarity, tolerance and respect – and the reality of party membership. I feel I need to make a stand for decency in our politics and as such I have decided to leave Labour.

When I stood down as chair of Stroud Green branch in February 2018 I was overwhelmed by the kindness shown by so many members. Their words of thanks, encouragement and understanding meant so much to me. It showed me, and I still believe this, that most members are idealistic and not ideological. I had hoped that my very public resignation would encourage the activists who had harangued me out of office to reconsider their behaviour. Unfortunately they just became more resolute. At the very next branch meeting I was described as having had a "breakdown" and that I was "mentally unstable". This was nothing more than gaslighting.

The hostility shown to me for not appearing sufficiently loyal to you, for trying to maintain a broad church membership and for having friends who were “Blairites” (real or imagined) is just one example of the toxic culture that has consumed the Labour party locally and nationally.

In July last year I was saddened that our mutual friend Russell Smith-Becker had resigned from the party. I was appalled by the reaction to Russell’s decision from people claiming to be your supporters on Facebook. Much of it was conspiratorial and some of it was overtly antisemitic. He was told to “f*** off”, accused of resigning to prevent criticism of Israel and asked how he would spend his "thirty pieces of silver".

In May last year I attended the General Committee of Hornsey and Wood Green CLP where an activist said that tweets from the Labour Friends of Israel Twitter account are “sent by an Israeli embassy staffer or from Jerusalem". Despite its clear conspiratorial antisemitic connotations the chair did not challenge or rebuke the activist. Likewise, we allowed candidates to stand in the recent local elections despite them defending the use of the Neo Nazi term “Zio” and sharing an article that concluded "Enough is enough. Fuck you all. Chag Pesach sameach".

Instead of listening to the concerns raised by Jewish Labour Movement delegates and local Rabbis, Hornsey and Wood Green CLP then voted overwhelmingly in favour of "affiliating" to Jewish Voice for Labour. It seemed a deliberately provocative act towards our local Jewish community. JVL is an organisation established for the sole purpose to obfuscate and apologise for antisemitism within the Labour party.

Over the past eighteen months, slowly but surely, all of my Jewish friends have left Labour. On the 18th February, Luciana Berger MP resigned from the party. The examples of abuse that Luciana has spoken about are truly dreadful and your lack of action to tackle the abuse is shameful. It is beyond belief that for fourteen months you have refused to meet with her. Her bravery and dignity has shown me that the time has come for me to resign my membership.

For me, your promises to tackle antisemitism have meant nothing whilst Chris Williamson has seemingly been given free rein to troll the Jewish community over the past three years. How have we become a party where a Jewish MP leaves because of antisemitic bullying and yet another MP has licence to go around the country supporting those who deploy anti-Semitic tropes and conspiracy theories?

The Jewish Labour Movement wrote to the Chief Whip in August 2018 raising their concerns about Chris Williamson and yet in January this year you described him as "a very good MP". I appreciate that he has now been suspended from the party. However, *The Independent* has reported that you personally intervened to prevent the whip being removed.

The culture of antisemitism did not start with Chris Williamson, although his roadshows and media appearances have certainly amplified it, and it will not end with his suspension. Especially as his suspension appears to have been made under such extreme duress and because his comments in Sheffield were greeted with applause from the activists present.

Antisemitism has been normalised in Labour and your behaviour over a number of years has legitimised it. Your friendships with conspiracy pedlars, Holocaust deniers and revisionists as well as supporters of antisemitic terror groups like Hezbollah gives credibility to their ideas and philosophies.

I look back at the written reports you provided when I was a General Committee delegate in Islington North and see that all the meetings and interviews with these conspiracists and racists are documented. And I wonder why we took no notice of this behaviour at that time. I can only conclude that we saw you as an irrelevance and your activities anachronistic. Unfortunately you are no longer an irrelevance. You are leader of the Labour party. You and your coterie of ideologues and aristo-Stalinists have created an institutional culture where antisemitism thrives. It has been brought from the fringe of the party to the forefront of the party.

I believe that you have said and done things that are clearly antisemitic. Your defence of the mural and the numerous recordings of you that have been brought to the public's attention in recent months provide sufficient evidence.

I came close to leaving the party when the video emerged of you saying that "[British Zionists] having lived in this country for a very long time, probably all their lives, they don't understand English irony either."

I believe that you were using "Zionist" as a euphemism for "Jew". I find it impossible to interpret it any other way. Page twelve of the Chakrabarti Report details how "Zionist" is used abusively as a euphemism for "Jew". This use of language is inexcusable. You were saying that Jewish people are un-British. They are the "other". These comments would not be tolerated if directed at any other minority group. I was so upset by what you said that I wrote to the party's Compliance Unit. I am yet to receive any acknowledgement. I stayed in the party at that time only because Cllr Richard Watts and Cllr David Poyser intervened to assure me that they did not believe you were an antisemite and that you were doing all you could to tackle antisemitism.

The lack of empathy shown by the Labour leadership and activists to Luciana Berger's resignation has lead me to conclude that the Labour party is institutionally antisemitic. Ian

Lavery's *Guardian* article (21/2/19), the reaction from your media surrogates and acolytes in the Parliamentary Party, Young Labour's tweets and retweets and your own belligerent video to members could not have been further from the listening exercise that was promised. Labour has become the nasty party.

The threats made by your supporters to Luciana Berger's unborn child. The threat by one of your supporters to Joan Ryan that she should be "shoved right back in the ovens". The motions at Hackney North CLP, Hastings and Rye CLP, Sheffield Hallam CLP, and now Alexandra branch in Hornsey and Wood Green CLP all express the belief that Jewish members of the party and the Jewish community are acting in bad faith. That Jews and their allies are lying about anti-Semitism. This is not a few bad apples. This is institutional. And now *The Observer* reports that you and your senior staff have intervened in disciplinary cases to protect those accused of antisemitism.

As David Hirsh, the UK's leading academic authority on antisemitism, recently wrote "Antisemitism threatens Jews but it is also always an indicator of the ascendency of an anti-democratic political culture".

In 2014 you laid a wreath in honour of Black September and the terrorists that organised the murder of eleven Israeli athletes at the Munich Olympics. Less than thirty years after the horror of the Holocaust, Jews were once again being murdered on German soil. Not just murdered but tortured. Castrated. It took place on the most prominent global stage, the Olympics. It left deep scars. So to commemorate those that masterminded these killings was grossly insensitive.

In August last year you asked members and the general public to believe you when you said you had not done so. Even though you were photographed doing it. Even though you had written about laying the wreath in the *Morning Star*. Your response to the public outrage was truly Orwellian. We were told to reject the evidence of our eyes and ears.

This anti-democratic political culture did not exist in Labour before you were elected leader. We see it in how pluralism and debate are being minimised in the party. Any difference of opinion among local members is seen as an attack on you, the great leader. Likewise, it can also been seen in how long it took you to listen to members and accept our conference policy on a second referendum, and yet it only took you a couple hours to decide that Hezbollah should not be proscribed in the UK. So many of my friends were so enthused by your leadership pitch in 2015 because you said members would be more involved in policy-making. The reality is far from this.

I had the great privilege to work on the general election campaign in the West Midlands in 2010. There I saw the transformational impact that a Labour government had across Birmingham and the Black Country. It also showed me how ingrained poverty and deprivation are in some of our communities and how fragile they would be under the pressures of austerity. I was heartbroken when Labour lost in 2010 and I am heartbroken that our communities have been subjected to the past nine years of cuts.

I walk under the bridge at Finsbury Park station twice a day on the way to and from work. Half a dozen people regularly sleep there at night. Seeing them there I feel a deep sense of shame. The Labour party, by being out of government, has failed them. Your leadership, by creating an institutional culture that prizes ideology over action, has failed them. I want Labour to be a party that delivers the radical change needed after almost a decade of austerity. I want Labour to house the homeless and help address their complex needs. I cannot see that happening while the leadership, activists and apparatus of the party are so consumed by hate and outright crankery.

My daughter has a book called *Fantastically Great Women Who Changed the World*. It has a chapter about Anne Frank. Every time we read it, without fail, my daughter asks me, “was Anne Frank brave?” And I always tell her that yes she was brave. I cannot read those pages and teach my daughter about what Anne Frank endured and her legacy if I remain a member of an institutionally antisemitic political party. I would be a hypocrite if I did. The only decent thing to do is for me to resign.

Richard Horton

2nd April 2019
Councillor Allan Barclay
Hartlepool

To: Jeremy Corbyn Leader of the Labour Party
Tom Watson Deputy Leader of the Labour Party
Fiona Stanton Regional Director of Labour North

Resignation as a member of the Labour Party

I would like to inform you of my resignation from the Labour Party with immediate effect.
The Labour Party has become embattled with infighting and is now taking a dangerous path. My fear has become a reality that the Labour Party has indeed become a party of antisemitism. It is my belief that the Labour Party has become the Nasty Party. I strongly believe the Labour Party should be fighting for working class people and those who are vulnerable in society and not fighting each other.
I first got involved in the Labour Party at fourteen years of age, leafleting, door-knocking and campaigning. Having served my country in the Royal Engineers for over 24 years I have always upheld my socialist values; this included supporting struggling families in the miners' strikes. Having left the army as a sergeant I joined the Labour Party in the early 1990s. I feel the Labour Party is now unrecognisable compared to when I first joined.

As an Armed Forces veteran I fear the Labour Party is at a dark turning point and marching towards fascism at a steady pace. I have witnessed antisemitism, racism, homophobia, disability discrimination and a general disrespect towards others. I am increasingly concerned that Labour North and the national leadership has seen examples and received complaints in relation to Hartlepool Labour members and done nothing to address this. You will all be aware that some cases have been reported over fifteen months ago and no acknowledgment or effort has been taken to address this. I feel Labour North has been complicit in this illegal and unacceptable behaviour. I fear that should Jeremy Corbyn and Jennie Formby not deal with this issue and should Labour secure a victory in Parliament then we will see dark times ahead and return to fascism like in the 1930s and 1940s.

Hartlepool is at a knife edge of turning its fortunes around. For the first time in over a generation the Council leader and Deputy Leader along with good council officers have attracted multi millions of pounds into Hartlepool. In real terms this means local jobs. This investment and hard work is at risk by Labour Councillors and members who are more interested in playing divisive political games and undermining the Labour administration they are part of. As a senior councillor I am aware that investors are very uneasy about the unwarranted criticism of the Council. I condemn the spiteful behaviour of some Labour Councillors who put their own self-serving behaviour and greed to become part of the leadership, rather than thinking about the town.

I am aware Labour North and the national leadership are aware of an incident where our council leader was physically threatened by Labour Party members and also vilified in a campaign meeting for being gay. The sentiment of the discussion was the Labour Party cannot be lead into future elections by gay people. I am distressed and worried that no action has been taken to address this kind of behaviour. I have also seen complaints made where an officer of the party has referred to Jewish people as dirty rats, black members of parliament being racially abused and the Holocaust being denied. With no will by the Labour Party to address such issues I have no other option but to resign my position from the Labour Party. Again Labour North and the national leadership of the party have seen complaints and again failed to act.

The Labour Party has been infiltrated by people who do not have true labour values at heart. It is normal behaviour in Hartlepool Labour Party for Corbynites to verbally abuse, jeer, hiss and boo at those who have a different view. This behaviour is not challenged within the meeting and has become normalised and encouraged. I was disappointed to learn Corbynites cheered and celebrated the resignation by Paul Beck from the Labour Party. Paul was a well -liked and respected Councillor who people connected with, a charity champion and a fellow Armed Forces veteran. Losing people like Paul Beck tells us that the Labour Party has a serious problem.

Jeremy Corbyn is the local party's biggest problem. Support is haemorrhaging due to Corbyn's leadership and true labour voters do not recognise a reason to support labour. I feel Jeremy Corbyn must resign in order for the Labour Party to become a respectable party.

I represent the Manor House Ward and am saddened that the National Party along with local Corbynites are destroying true labour values. Residents need a socialist party who will stand up for them and not concentrate on infighting and personal attacks. Sadly the Labour Party has lost its way and risks the hard work carried out in my ward by Stephen Akers-Belcher and Marjorie James. We have worked well as a team, united on tackling child and family poverty, improving the environment and introducing improved parking. This work is at risk by an unpleasant minority.

The last straw was the total contempt Corbyn has shown towards the Armed Forces and his view that soldiers should be prosecuted as a result of their service to our country. My former commanding officer was murdered in cold blood in Bielefeld, West Germany some 39 years ago

because of his previous service in NI and no government has acted to bring his assassin to justice. Corbyn's contempt demonstrates a lack of respect for those who have served in the Armed Forces and their families.
It is a very sad day for me after almost 52 years of service to the Labour Party that it has come to my resignation from the party, but I feel I have no alternative.
Please ensure my contact details are removed from the Labour Party database.

Councillor Allan Barclay

3rd April 2019
Merilyn Davies
Former Labour District Councillor

Media Statement
I could not have been prouder to be elected, a year ago, as a Labour and Co-op councillor for Hanborough and Freeland.
But in that year, my party has changed, and whilst I know my former Labour councillors at West Oxfordshire District Council share my values and commitment to our communities, I have come to the conclusion to stay in the party would make me complicit in the antisemitism and climate of hate and fear now generated across CLPs.
I believe the Labour Party is now institutionally antisemitic. It is not just those who generate it who are to blame but those that stand by silent while they do. I can no longer be silent. I will be louder.

7th April 2019
Email to Constituency Labour Party

Dear All,
As some time has now passed I wanted to explain to you my reasons for resigning so abruptly from the Labour Party this week.
As you know I have struggled for a while now with the antisemitism in the Labour Party as well as the increasingly hostile environment on the CLP

FB page. I believe the Labour Party is now institutionally antisemitic – in that the structures members operate under have become antisemitic as opposed to all members being so – and whilst I found this an abhorrent situation I remained a member because I felt I was best placed to tackle this from the inside. I also couldn't bear to leave the party I was so proud to represent or the family I felt I had in the CLP.
When I posted the Gordon Brown video it was almost instantly removed after X made a comment which made it clear X thought it was inappropriate. I fully understand the reason why it was removed and appreciate this was done with the best of intentions. The fact remains, however, that we have allowed a small group of people to dictate the narrative by remaining silent and deleting things which cause them to react. X did not like that video because it supported Jews and the JLM. This is because X feels antisemitism is being used to smear Corbyn and that Jews are weaponising it. Whilst it is true some may seize on the opportunity to beat Corbyn with antisemitism it is also overwhelmingly the case that Jews feel threatened, targeted and isolated by the behaviour of some in the party. When it was removed I asked X and X to re-instate it and agreed to leave it until the next day for the issue to be resolved. I then asked the Labour Group for their support in the matter as it was something I felt very strongly about. There are, I'm sure,

various versions of what came next but for me, the lack of support was the final straw. I had previously asked the group to be signatories to a letter asking the JLM to remain in the Labour Party. I received no reply. To be again ignored was hurtful and I felt undermined and as if my passions didn't matter. I support many passions of other Cllrs, badgers, the Cogges Surgery, young care leavers, when I don't always share those passions (X, I have to admit it, I hate badgers!) but do so because I'm passionate about those of you who are. I came to the conclusion the reason I wasn't being supported in my passion was because it would mean becoming the target of those such as X. It's easier to support badgers, but Jews need our voices too. They need to hear we stand with them.

The combination of the reaction to X's responses to the GB post – and the fear of his anger being more important than offering support to Jewish people – and the lack of support from group meant I left. I did so angrily and I apologise for that. Since then I have worked with X and X to manage the situation in the media and I have remained as silent as I can so as not to hamper the amazing efforts for May. I have hidden posts made by CLP members on my FB post so as not to highlight the issues in the CLP membership and I have also stressed that whilst I can no longer support the Labour leadership I fully support the local candidates and believe they are as

committed and dedicated to their residents as I am.
In return, I have been told I am being paid by Israel, that I support the murder of Palestinian children, I am unhinged, a liar, deceitful and much more, some of this from members of the CLP. I understand people' hurt and anger, but I was once part of your family too. I worked hard to champion Labour in West Oxfordshire and was proud to do so. I have no wish to be an independent. I stood to bring labour values to the people of Hanborough and Freeland, I sought media coverage just so I could see those words in print and remind everyone that was my purpose for working for them. Being an independent says what? Nothing. There is no longer a message I am bringing people and no greater society in West Oxfordshire I am trying to build. I am alone and what can I achieve for them through that? It remains to be seen if I can stay on as a Cllr but as much as I love the core of the CLP and the hard work and values it brings to the people it represents, I could no longer represent the national party without feeling a sense of shame. I tried to reconcile the local with the national but in the end it turns out they are linked by a greater degree than I could accept.
Finally, it has been made clear I would not be welcomed back, and I accept that. I would ask, however, for you to consider at some point in the future how very lonely and isolating it is to no

longer be part of the Labour family and that whilst you may disagree with my actions or how I went about them, for a long time we shared that family together. I thank X, X, X, X, X and X for understanding that and reaching out to check on me as well as the numerous welfare checks I received from other WODC Cllrs. It is a small area – especially my village – and so has been daunting even going to the local Co-op, and I dreaded going into Witney on Saturday, so I thank you X for the hug you gave me when I visited the stall.

Merilyn Davies

3rd April 2019
Councillor Jason Fojtik
Clopton

Statement on Facebook

It is with deep regret that I am resigning from the Labour Party.
I joined the Labour Party in 2010 because the Labour Government had transformed the lives of families in my community over the previous 13 years by improving public services and offering greater opportunities.
In 2015, I was proud to be elected as Town and District Councillor for Clopton Ward in Stratford Upon Avon, the first Labour win in the town since 1974. This is the place I grew up and live in. I have worked hard over the last four years to address the many challenges that face the local community and am always available to help my constituents.
I would like to continue to serve my community on the Town and District Councils but after careful consideration have concluded that I can no longer do that under the current Labour leadership. The Labour Party today is no longer the Party I joined, following the election of Jeremy Corbyn it has become a hostile environment for anyone questioning Leadership policy. I, and many other long-term members, who have served as officers and councillors, have

been subjected to abuse and bullying, made to feel that we are no longer welcome in the Party. I have stood up to this and am grateful to many friends and colleagues who have provided support but there comes a point when enough is enough.

I am resigning for two main reasons.

Firstly, racism, in the form of antisemitism, in the Labour Party has appalled me. I tabled a motion at full council meeting for adoption of the internationally recognised definition of antisemitism as policy, I won support from cross party. For months the Labour Party failed to act before finally being shamed into accepting the definition, but little has changed and I have come to the conclusion that a Party that has always been proud of its anti-racism, has become institutionally antisemitic under Jeremy Corbyn's leadership. Ignoring this deplorable behaviour by our supporters is tantamount to tacit endorsement.

Secondly, I am and always have been a passionate supporter of the European Union. The Labour Party I joined was an internationalist party that valued the contribution of all including EU citizens. Instead of wholly backing the Remain cause the Labour leadership has obfuscated and distorted on this issue leaving millions in despair. The Labour leader failed to attend the largest demonstration in a generation in London to call for a Peoples Vote and has tolerated Shadow

Ministers who have defied whips and Party policy to oppose it.
Brexit will do enormous damage to the economy of Stratford Upon Avon, particularly the manufacturing, services and tourism that local jobs depend on. I cannot remain a member of a Party which supports and enables Brexit which came about purely as a split within the Conservative party. Any form of Brexit will harm opportunities for young people, jobs, working conditions and our NHS. The people Labour represents - those we give voice to - are the ones who will be harmed most. It is an act of utter betrayal and dogmatic ignorance by Jeremy Corbyn to support, and not oppose vigorously, this act of catastrophic national self-harm.
I came into politics to change society for the better, to win the opportunity to serve. My values have not changed. I did not come into politics to spend my time and energy fighting people in the same party. Pointless squabbles which detract from the real issues at hand, fighting austerity and collectively working to overthrow the Tories. The racism, factionalism, bullying and intolerance of any dissenting view is intolerable. It has ceased to be the broad church I joined. I despair at what the Party I have devoted a decade of my life has become, and the far left doctrines and dogmas that now constrict it.
I respect all those true and valued friends and colleagues who will stay as members, but it is

with enormous sadness that I must resign my membership of the party.
I feel I still have much to offer to public service and to the residents of Clopton and to the town that I am very proud of and therefore will be standing in the forthcoming Council elections as an Independent Candidate.
My values and aspirations have not changed in that time and nor will they but now, like others, I must find another means by which to realise those values, deliver better lives for the people in my community who need the best of representation and help give others the opportunity to serve.

Councillor Jason Fojtik

12th May 2019
Bridget Prentice
Member of Parliament for Lewisham East 1992-2010

Karie Murphy
Acting General Secretary
The Labour Party

Dear Karie

I have been a member of the Labour party for 45 years. For over half of that time, I was an elected representative of the Party whether at branch or CLP level, in local government as a councillor and as the Member of Parliament for Lewisham East in Opposition and as a Minister in the most successful Labour Government in our history.
It is with the deepest sadness and some anger, that I resign from the party as it is presently formed as it no longer represents the values, aspirations or vision that led me to join it so many years ago.
I shall outline a few areas where the response from the leadership has fallen short.
Everyone in a leadership position has a duty to lead. Yet in all the major issues of the day, you have called it wrong.
Over the past three years I have watched in horror as Jewish members have begged for support against the growth of antisemitism both

within and out with the Party. Mealy-mouthed words have replaced what should have been strong and determined condemnation of the bigots and bullies. The response was slow, reluctant and inadequate. Even when complaints were upheld, the punishment was often no more than a slap on the wrist. If we are a Party of social justice, equality and fairness that was not leadership. For a pregnant woman MP to be bullied out of the party is shameful and embarrassing.

It is easy to say Jeremy is not racist. But there is the sin of omission. By not standing up to the bullies and the antisemites, by not standing shoulder to shoulder with comrades who were being vilified and trolled through social media, whose lives were threatened and families under stress, Jeremy showed no leadership. Leaders stand up to be counted. They root out the evil; they show that such racism will not be tolerated. They don't twist and turn to find ways of keeping their supporters on board when those self- same supporters have been shown to be racist, antisemitic and bullies. The whitewash that was the Chakrabarti Report should have been a signal that this leadership was either incapable of leading or prepared to accept racists and bullies as long as they were their racists and bullies.

It's clear to any objective observer that Jeremy has no wish to remain in Europe; that in his limited thinking, Europe is 'a bad thing', apparently completely ignorant of the benefits it has brought to working people in this country to say nothing of the internationalist outlook any half decent Socialist ought to express. To use European workers as the cause of lower wages for indigenous workers is as disgraceful as it is pandering to the baser views of racists.

I have come to the conclusion he not only did not campaign vigorously for the Labour Party's position on Remain but where he could, he undermined it. (The notorious 7 out of 10 interview springs to mind) If the suggestion that Labour party information had been passed on to the Leave campaign is true that simply adds to the belief that every effort was made to undermine the party's policy. The recent comments about the local elections telling the major parties to deliver Brexit would be laughable if it were not so palpably wrong and pathetic. The damage to this country and most importantly to the poorest, the most vulnerable, the dispossessed, the underclass – all those that the Labour Party was born to protect – will be devastating. That Jeremy and those of you around him either cannot see that, or feel justified in disregarding it because of a narrow ideological pursuit, flies in the face of the moral right to lead a party which wants to transform the lives of those most in need.

Which brings me to the cult. I joined the Labour Party, not a cult. Singing 'Oh Jeremy Corbyn' at

Glastonbury might be mildly amusing but the inability to countenance any criticism of The Leader is not. Never in my life in the Party has a Leader not been criticised, questioned, asked to justify a position – and rightly so. But that's not allowed under the Corbyn Cult. Anyone questioning the leadership's position is vilified; complaints sent in to the disciplinary panel like something out of a North Korean rulebook that disloyalty to the leader is a criminal offence.
Anyone praising the successes of the last Labour Government – worse still invoking the name of our most successful Prime Minister, Tony Blair, - is condemned as a Red Tory. The biggest insult is to be condemned as a Blairite – I *am* a Blairite and proudly so but Tom Watson a Blairite? Don't make me laugh. That's weakness. That's not leadership.
But then, perhaps, I am still thinking the Labour Party is supposed to be a democratic socialist party, a broad church. Funny how those of us who are Blairites and others, like Tom, could live with the Jeremies and Dianas and John Mc Donnells in the party but somehow in three years that broad church has narrowed its aisles so that there is no room for those other than the cult venerating the messiah. And when the cult clutches the Good Friday Agreement to its bosom as the work of the sainted Jeremy, you insult the life and courage of my good friend Mo Mowlam. She showed leadership.

So let's look at that membership. Jeremy won on a wave of enthusiasm, even idealism. I have friends who voted for him. But instead of harnessing that enthusiasm and idealism for the greater good – as Clem Attlee or Keir Hardie would have done – it has been deliberately ignored on the one issue that unites the majority of young people in the UK today – remaining in the EU. So many of those young people were on the People's March two months ago. Where was Jeremy? In Lancaster ostensibly campaigning for the local elections – we lost seats there. When issues that directly affect people in this country but the answers don't sit cosily with the ideology, he's not there. Like Macavity. Yet he can attend marches, show solidarity with regimes which are murdering their people, harassing women and LGBT communities and destroying their economies. That's not leadership. The talk was of giving the party back to the membership. In fact it is run by a familial clique with the members' views being wilfully ignored because they do not align with the blinkered view of those at the top of the organisation.

That the EHRC feels it needs to investigate the Labour party for antisemitism – an organisation we set up in the face of fury from the right – is shameful; that women MPs have been bullied out of the party by racists and thugs is shameful; that the leadership continues to fudge on Europe is shameful; that the rules of the party have been

changed deny the democracy that so many thought would come with Jeremy is shameful. It is not leadership.
There are good people in the Labour Party – here in Lewisham East a hard working MP, a campaigning team around her and a sound and campaigning and innovative council all being constantly undermined by the narrow ideological path tramped by the clique at the head of the party. And of course I am sad at leaving them – many worked for me and for Heidi Alexander over so many years. They are good people. And I understand why so many of those thoughtful, good democratic socialists feel they should stay and fight and win the party back.
But the party has been destroyed. It is no longer the party of Hardie and Attlee and Blair. It is no longer the party that upholds the values of social justice and fairness in our society and an open and welcoming view of the world. This is no longer the Labour Party. You should change its name.

Former MP Bridget Prentice

24th May 2019
Mary Honeyball
Labour MEP 2000-2019
Announced Evening Standard
Leadership is out of kilter and that's why I'm leaving

Now that the MEP votes are safely cast, I feel able to announce my decision to leave the Labour Party.

It has not been easy. A Labour Party member for 43 years, I thought I would stay in what was until recently my political and spiritual home until the day I died. For 27 of those 43 years I was an elected representative - eight years as a London Borough councillor and later I spent almost two decades in the European Parliament.

Sadly, as I stand down as a London MEP and retire from elected politics, I feel I can no longer remain in the Party which nurtured me and gave me unrivalled opportunities.

Labour's stance on Brexit is just one symptom of what has become the party's real problem. The Labour Party, my party, which once stood for social democracy, produced reforming governments and legislated for the many not the few, has been comprehensively hijacked not only by the hard left but also by fellow travellers who

appear to support the views of the Communist Party. The takeover appears irreversible for the foreseeable future. The National Executive Committee has fallen and I believe there are people working in the Leader of the Opposition's office who have strong Communist Party links.
I do not make these accusations of Communist influence lightly. There is evidence from the Communists themselves that they are in agreement with Corbyn's policies. In a letter to the Guardian on 4 January Nick Wright, Communist Party of Great Britain head of communications, wrote, "Communists want a People's Brexit. Unconstrained by EU treaties, single market rules and directives, a left-led Labour government could develop a worker-led industrial strategy... and take the transport, energy and postal service profiteers back into public ownership."
This to me sounds suspiciously like Corbyn's programme. No concessions are made to economic reality and everything will be marvellous once Britain is out of the "neo-liberal EU". Corbyn has, in addition, regularly contributed to the Morning Star, the Communist Party newspaper.
Since the end of the Second World War until the election of Jeremy Corbyn as Labour leader, Communists and their sympathisers (fellow travellers) failed to make appreciable inroads into British politics. It has, however, been a different

matter in the trade unions, who are still major Labour Party funders and important players in policy making. During the early 1980s I worked for one of the civil service unions which has now been merged into a much larger organisation. Despite the overwhelming majority of my union members being moderate in their opinions, the national executive committee and other key positions were run by Communists and fellow travellers. They achieved this by appearing reasonable while organising behind the scenes by, for example, holding caucuses prior to meetings. The results of these Communist labours were not always obvious, but they did give rise to support for strange causes such as Cuba Solidarity together with a policy of either appointing Communist Party members as paid officials or trying to get them to support the Communist line once they had taken up post. For me, what I perceived to the most difficult aspect was the Communists' complete denial of parliamentary democracy. To me, they seemed to not believe in democratic elections for either parliament or government. The preferred route, as far as I could tell, was revolution.

The Communist Party and its fellow travellers hated, and probably still hate, the Labour Party. In the early 1980s, the period when Thatcherism was beginning to take off, the union's quasi-Communist establishment would talk about how the previous Labour government had cut public services in almost the same breath as Thatcher's plans to abolish secondary picketing. It was very much a plague on both your houses even though the Labour house was much nearer to their own point of view than the Conservatives. This kind of attitude, I believe, informed Jeremy Corbyn's serial rebellions against previous Labour governments.

Between 1997 and 2010, Corbyn voted against the Labour whip, essentially voting against the Labour government, 428 times. When Labour was in government he was consistently the most rebellious MP. Corbyn shared a platform with leaders of the IRA while the troubles were raging in Northern Ireland. He has over the years shown a strong hostility to the West and the United States. He is anti-NATO and has been sympathetic to Hezbollah and Hamas.

The antisemitism currently infecting the Labour Party, I believe, derives from the Labour Leadership's animosity towards Israel primarily because the country is an ally of the United States. Although the state of Israel and the Jewish people are two completely different things, Corbyn and his allies appear to see fit to view them as virtually one and the same. Shamefully, the Labour Leadership have done nothing like enough to purge the Labour Party of the racism shown towards its Jewish members.

The main reason I am leaving Labour is, of course, the Party's disastrous stance on Brexit. Jeremy

Corbyn is, at best, perceived as sitting on the fence over membership of the European Union. For most of his life, Corbyn has been a committed Eurosceptic, and there is no real evidence to show that he has changed his mind. Many in the Shadow Cabinet and the majority of the ruling National Executive Committee agree with the Leader. Labour now has an impossible policy designed to appeal to both remainers and leavers. One of my personal guiding political convictions is that Britain's place is at the heart of Europe, leading and reforming the EU from within. Now I am no longer a Labour representative I cannot in all conscience support a Party whose leadership is so out of kilter with my own fundamental principles.

I do not for the time being intend to join another political party. I will watch and possibly wait to see if Labour can cast off the hard left and the fellow travellers and regain its standing as a democratic, outward looking party. It gives me no pleasure to see a once great organisation succumb to an anti-democratic and potentially totalitarian ideology.

Former MEP Mary Honeyball

8th July 2019

THE VIEW FROM SOMERSET

Susan Carlton

Labour supporter for 60 years

Open letter

Last July I attended a ward meeting of my local Labour party held in the small market town in Somerset near where I lived. It was around the time of the growing antisemitism row over the party's reluctance to agree to four of the terms of the International Holocaust Remembrance Alliance (IHRA) guidelines which had already been accepted in full by the UK, Scottish, Welsh governments, 124 local councils, the Crown Prosecution Service and many Jewish groups. On July 18th Margaret Hodge had publicly accused Jeremy Corbyn of being an antisemite. I had been disconcerted to read in the papers sent out in advance of the meeting, mention of 'special interests'. It did not take Sherlock Holmes powers of deduction to infer this might refer to 'Jewish interests'.

The meeting lasted about two hours and was totally different from any other Labour party meeting I have ever attended. I have voted Labour since October 1959 when I voted for Hugh Gaitskell in my school's mock election and, coming from a strongly Conservative supporting family, didn't dare tell my mother. I don't wish to romanticise the tenor of party meetings over the following years. Strong opinions had been expressed sincerely and often forcefully. Shouting was not unknown. But possibly because voting Labour in deepest Somerset is traditionally somewhat of a niche activity, I had always experienced a degree of camaraderie. But not on that occasion.

The phrase 'special interests' was picked up on from the start by the Chairman. He denounced any and all charges of antisemitism as coming from people under the direct manipulation of the State of Israel purely designed to advance the agenda of the Israeli government. No evidence was produced. He then declared that such accusations obviously stemmed solely from a desire to attack Jeremy Corbyn made by people clearly acting as Israeli puppets. These individuals' motives were to harm the party and sow dissent. Again, no evidence was put forward in support of these pronouncements. I found his venomous hatred of Israel shocking and his outraged defence of the party leader unconvincing. None of my fellow Labour party members challenged him. Nor did I. They all appeared convinced that this portrayal of the situation was self-evidently true falling into the... nobody could argue with... everybody knows... school of political analysis.

The discussion then opened out and three contributions were made from the floor. First along the lines of, 'What can you expect from the Jews? Always making trouble.' The second demanding, 'Why can't they stop going on about the Holocaust? It's such a long time ago.' And the third was someone shouting out, 'When are they going to stop killing little Palestinian babies?' I was stunned by this outpouring of aggression towards Jews, and this time one other person and I did try to speak, but I felt intimidated being on the receiving end of such hostility from a group of angry middle aged men and left as soon as I could. As I was walking back to my car to go home this one man followed me and we stood talking in the car park. 'Are you alright?' he asked, seeing I was upset. 'No, not really,' I replied.

Over the next few weeks whenever I talked about this meeting to my mainly Labour voting, if not party members, friends and family they seemed unsure how much to believe. After all, they puzzled, this was the Labour party and everyone knows Labour was non racist plus this was rural Somerset where Jews were almost unknown so what was all this about? Surely I was exaggerating?

On 11th February 2019 I received an email from an investigations officer of the central Labour party saying my complaint had been forwarded to him as part of a wider series of complaints, citing bullying and misogyny, made by a fellow member of my constituency Labour party. (This person had not attended the July meeting but had heard what had taken place from the only other person to have spoken out.) That same day I sent the party official an email itemising what had occurred. I also spoke to him by phone saying I wanted the matter investigated as part of the nearly 700 other outstanding complaints of antisemitism. He said he would get back to me. Over the following months I sent him a further four emails but heard nothing back concerning this complaint. On 23rd April I sent Tom Watson an email briefly outlining my complaint and received an instant response promising that he, or a member of his term, would respond within ten working days. On 13th May I sent him a further email suggesting it might be best not to make promises you don't keep. Again an automatic acknowledgement of my email but since then nothing.

On June 6th I received an email from the complaints' team of the Labour party apologising for the delay in responding due to the sharp increase in the number of complaints. They stated that my complaint had been fully investigated, was now closed and that due to legal obligations around data protection they were unable to disclose further information. Obviously I have no idea whether my complaint had indeed been fully investigated, just a little bit or had been deleted straight away with zero examination. I was convinced taking it further either with the central party or Tom Watson was a waste of time. So that, according to the complaints' department, was that. (My fellow party member who had made the first of five complaints on 17th March 2018, that is 16 months ago, has still to receive any response.)

I decided to go back over the things that had been said last July ago, cross-reference them to specific IHRA clauses defining antisemitism, determine if the two matched up and thus assess whether there was, at the very least, something of a case to answer. The IHRA guidelines had finally, albeit reluctantly, been adopted by the Labour party.

Using of the term special interests/'Making mendacious allegations about Jews manipulating the media.'

People acting under the manipulation of the state of Israel and working to advance the Israeli government's agenda/ 'Making demonising allegations about a worldwide Jewish conspiracy.'

Making unfounded attacks on Jeremy Corbyn demonstrated that Jews are Israeli puppets/ 'Accusing Jewish citizens of being more loyal to Israel, or to the alleged priorities of Jews worldwide, than to the interests of their own nation.'

What can you expect from the Jews? Always making trouble/'Using images associated with classical antisemitism.'

Still going on about the Holocaust/ 'Accusing the Jews as a people of exaggerating the Holocaust.'

Killing little Palestinian babies/ 'Holding Jews collectively responsible for the actions of the state of Israel.'

That looks to me like grounds for a case. Words casually chucked out and insults thrown around do matter. Even in bucolic Somerset.

Over the last year there has been a 16% increase in antisemitic hate crime rising from 1,420 reported incidents in 2017 to 1,652 in 2018. Death threats to Jewish MPs have been made, armed security for synagogues, Jewish schools and institutions has increased and attacks both physical and verbal on Jews going about their daily lives have risen. Obviously not all of this can be laid at any one door but multiple instances of party leaders and officials, Labour MPs, senior union representatives, ordinary party members tweeting and re-tweeting offensive language, pictures, cartoons and 'jokes' can no longer be ignored but have become almost normalised. And the just a few rotten apples argument only goes so far.

The question arises of why the increase in antisemitism in the Labour party has happened now? Britain has a tradition of persecuting Jews dating back many centuries but also a history of accepting mass Jewish immigration. Commerce, medicine, law, universities, music, literature, journalism, theatre, film and television, amongst many other fields, have benefitted from Jewish talents so what has changed? The stupid and snobbish prejudices of my childhood have decreased if not entirely disappeared, only to be replaced by something far more pernicious. Peering at the centre from the distant provinces it can seem as if the current secretive inner cabal of the Labour party holds an ideologically obsessive, almost fundamentalist, loathing of the capitalist system both in this country and even more so of the triumphalist neo-liberal variety flaunted by the reviled United States. Any alliance between the dominance of Trump's America and the long established trans-national finances of Jews, personified by the fabulously rich extended Rothschild family, is singled out for particular vilification. Add to this stew the fact that the Jewish state of Israel is America's greatest ally in the Middle East and there is, in this analysis, ample ammunition for attacking Jews. And despite the fact that many British Jews are highly critical of the Netanyahu government and particularly scandalised by the settlements' programme, they all share, according to this thesis, an equal responsibility with every Israeli citizen for killing Palestinian babies. Step by step by step, and recklessly risking the destruction of the party along the way, the connections have been made.

It is for these reasons that despite my nearly sixty years as a supporter, the friendships, the canvassing (usually in the rain), standing as a councillor, the shared purpose to make society just that bit better I feel I must resign my membership. And that inevitably includes losing my vote and annual subscription. I no longer wish to be associated with a political party so riddled with racism which refuses to accept, either through malice or indifference, that there is a serious problem. There comes a moment when standing on the side lines wringing my hands shades into collusion. To parrot Theresa May, racism means racism and today some in the Labour party appear to have adopted a pick 'n mix position: they really like black people, are pretty keen on brown people, just can't stand Jews. And so, with all that in mind, if I were to be asked the same question by the guy in the car park, which I was asked last July, as to whether I was alright I would have to reply, 'No. I feel terrible.'

From the very highest level of the party – with the election of Lisa Forbes as MP for Peterborough and her accompanying baggage of antisemitic insults, to the on-off fiasco around allowing Chris Williamson back into the party – down to the grassroots level of local ward meetings, this malaise pervades. And now in a development with potentially hugely damaging consequences for the party's reputation, the Equalities and Human Rights Commission (EHRC) has launched a formal investigation into the existence of antisemitism within the Labour party. Falling into a similar category as the BNP is a truly dreadful position to be in. I hope to be able to re-join the party in the future when it moves on from sanctimonious whining and unfulfilled promises to a radical commitment to finally deal with this shameful episode in our history.

And, for what it's worth, I'm not Jewish.

Susan Carlton

9th July 2019
Lord David Triesman
Former Government Minister and General Secretary Labour Party

Dear Angela,

I am resigning from the Whip with immediate effect. It is a painful decision arrived at with great sadness. My commitment to the party has been a central plank of my political life and I treasure the experience of having served as the General Secretary.

But the decision has become inevitable. Day by day the extent and depth of antisemitism become clearer in the top leadership and the National Executive Committee. Antisemites are shielded and solid and serious party members are thrown out unceremoniously. And each new manifestation is followed by a grim parade of social media messages directed at Jewish party members. The experience of life in the party has become sickening. Of course, there are many great friends with great ethics who find this as ugly as I do whether they are Jewish or not. There are many policies I will always support. I haven't changed ideologies.

However, we have slipped into the familiar gutter of so many of the hard left and the old tropes about the secret wiring connecting Jewish entrepreneurs and the use of wealth to exercise secretive control can be heard on an almost daily basis. For me, this has not been about Israel where I always set myself the benchmarks of compliance with international law. As a Foreign Minister I always criticised breaches of international law whatever the side, the Israeli government or those firing rockets at Israel and denying its right to exist. My decision is straightforwardly about the party leadership's use of any excuse to allow their allies to attack Jews or to engage with antisemites.

My sad conclusion is that the Labour Party is very plainly institutionally antisemitic, and its leader and his circle are antisemitic having never once made the right judgement call about an issue reflecting deep prejudice. The number of examples is shocking.

It is no longer a safe political environment for Jewish people or other opponents of antisemitism. It is time to recognise the reality. I always said it was worth hanging on to fight so long as there was a prospect of winning. I now don't believe with this leadership there is.

It is also impossible to take seriously a number of our policy positions. The vacillations on Brexit which have additionally encouraged xenophobia and undermined our security and economic standing to the huge disadvantage of the British people, and the callow support for authoritarian leaders not least Putin show an extraordinarily disregard for the international security of our country. Our defence and our NATO postures are worse than ambiguous. It isn't responsible any longer to accept decisions on parliamentary conduct from those proposing to damage the UK in these ways.

I will continue to admire colleagues who feel they should struggle on. I respect their choice. It is very painful to step back from a lifetime of commitment. It is more comfortable to hope something will turn up to change it all and give impetus to the idea of clinging together in solidarity. It is, I fear, the 'Mr Micawber' option that however improbable something is bound to turn up. I'm sorry but to me this is the unicorn delusion. In politics things turn up if you create the conditions for their development.

We may one day be the party of anti-racism once again but it certainly isn't today.

Lord David Triesman
Secretary and Government Minister

9th July, 2019
Lord Leslie Turnberg

The Labour Party and its leadership are now so far removed from the party I joined that I fear that I can no longer take the whip.
My reasons include;-
Parliamentary democracy is ignored by the leadership. The Party is run by and for the 'machine' without reference to Parliament.
Public opinion is also ignored. No positive reaction has followed the disastrous results of the recent elections. Wider democracy is thus ignored as the National Executive believe they know best.
The top of the party has lurched to the extreme Left and are now in a commanding position. It is now difficult to see how they can be dislodged.
These problems are compounded by a lack of direction, no clear manifesto commitments to the policies that those of us in Labour hold so dear and the damaging vacillation over Brexit by our Leader.
Foreign policy is leading us to disaster. Anti-American and pro-Russian and Venezuelan policies will prove not only a severe security risk they will damage our economy and social well-being.
The antisemitic accusations hanging round the neck of the party are particularly shameful and leading to wide sections of the public, not only amongst the Jews, believing that it is a racist

party. Our leader's antizionist attitude goes well beyond any legitimate criticism of the Israeli Government and into a denial of Israel's right to exist. He suggests that Balfour was a huge mistake and should be rescinded. He fails to recognize that as antisemitism rises it ensures that Jews become more rather than less Zionistic as they look to Israel as a safe home. Antizionism has become the new antisemitism.

I am well aware of the sense of comradeship and brotherhood that has sustained me in the Lords and been such a delight over the last 20 years. It is therefore with considerable pain, sorrow and reluctance that I take the step of resigning the Whip. But it is the impossible conditions I have outlined above and the belief that there is no possibility of any change in our leadership for some time to come that give me no option but to take this step.

Lord Leslie Turnberg

16TH October 2019
Dame Louise Ellman
Member of Parliament Liverpool Riverside 1997-2019

Dame Louise on Twitter: 'I have made the truly agonising decision to leave the Labour Party after 55 years. I can no longer advocate voting Labour when it risks Corbyn becoming PM.'

Dame Louise Ellman's Statement
I have this evening resigned from the Labour Party. I have been a member for 55 years and a public representative in local and central government continuously since 1970. My decision has been truly agonising, as it has been for the thousands of other party members who have already left.
I will not join any other party. I hope that under different leadership I will be able to return to my political home. I would like to thank the overwhelming majority of Labour MPs who have fought Labour's antisemitism valiantly and the Co-operative Party who have taken a firm and unequivocal stance against this racism. I would also like to applaud the integrity of those local members who have continued to speak out.
I believe that Jeremy Corbyn is not fit to serve as our Prime Minister. With a looming general election and the possibility of him becoming Prime Minister, I feel I have to take a stand. I

cannot advocate a government led by Jeremy Corbyn.

Under Jeremy Corbyn's leadership, antisemitism has become mainstream in the Labour Party. Jewish members have been bullied, abused and driven out. Antisemites have felt comfortable and vile conspiracy theories have been propagated. A party that permits anti-Jewish racism to flourish cannot be called antiracist.

This is not compatible with the Labour Party's values of equality, tolerance and respect for minorities. Shamefully, its anti-Jewish racism is now being investigated by one of the last Labour government's proudest creations, the Equality and Human Rights Commission.

Jeremy Corbyn – who spent three decades on the backbenches consorting with, and never confronting, antisemites, Holocaust deniers and terrorists – has attracted the support of too many antisemites.

The Labour Party is no longer a safe place for Jews and Jeremy Corbyn must bear the responsibility for this. We cannot allow him to do to the country what he has done to the Labour Party.

The overwhelming majority of the Jewish community is fearful of what a Corbyn government might mean for Britain's Jews. I share those concerns. But this issue is not simply about the Jewish community. This is about the nature of our society. Jeremy Corbyn's seeming tolerance of antisemitism would embolden racists, poison our public debate and damage the social cohesion of our country.

My values – traditional Labour values – have remained the same. It is Labour, under Jeremy Corbyn, that has changed. He has presided over a culture of hatred, fear and intolerance in the Labour Party.

But this issue is no longer just about the Labour Party – it is about the threat a Jeremy Corbyn premiership could pose to the country.

Dame Louise Ellman

PART 2

WHERE IS 2017?

There's a gap in these resignation letters. After Lord Parry Mitchell's of 21st September 2016 there isn't another until Judith Flacks-Leigh 19 months later in April 2018. After that there's a steady flurry beginning July 2018 and finishing with Dame Louise Ellman MP, 16th October 2019 after the announcement of the general election as this book was about to be published.
Reliable figures indicate that tens of thousands of members have left Labour since the peak of the Miliband £3 membership. I can only speculate that some of these must have been in 2017. I dug out just one but the writer didn't wish it to be published. If you're reading this and wish to share a resignation letter, so long as it's interesting and courteous I'll be happy to add it to the Facebook group, FORCED OUT.
You can look at the brief timeline and try to work it out for yourself. You can also read below what some of these knowledgeable people wrote back to me when I asked them about this space.
These further replies are interesting because each of the original letters was written at a different time; each person will not only have a different personal perspective but also a different historical one.

What all share is their loyalty to Labour values, which made them reluctant to lose hope. Because these follow up letters were written within days of each other, in the second week of November 2019, the reflections are immensely valuable.

So – why the Gap?

Lord Parry Mitchell
Judith I can only speculate.
In that 18 month period perhaps were hoping the situation would get better vis a vis Comrade Jez.
But it didn't and then perhaps they were stirred.
The fact is that people find it hard to resign from a political party especially Labour
Regards
Parry

Russell Smith-Becker
Dear Judith
I can't say why no-one resigned in 2017 over antisemitism (I'm sure some did, if not in your sample), so can only answer as to why I resigned when I did (July 2018).
There were, through 2016 and 2017, a number of high profile antisemitism cases (Ken Livingstone, Jackie Walker, etc).I found this very concerning, but at least some of those people were suspended and the party hierarchy said that it was trying to deal with the problem. In retrospect

it is clear that not enough was being done at that time, but I was living in hope that things would improve. I clung to this hope partly because the party had been a big part of my life for so long and partly in thinking that if I and others like me stayed then we might be able to influence the party to take antisemitism seriously.

Things then came to a head in spring 2018. Various disciplinary cases from the previous couple of years were still not dealt with. Christine Shawcroft was revealed to have supported a member who had supported a Holocaust denial post, and she had been the chair of the Disputes Sub-Committee. The Jewish Leadership Council and the Board of Deputies of British Jews - neither of which would usually get so far into politics - organised a demonstration in Parliament Square in March 2018. I attended this, and it is then that I felt forced to acknowledge to myself that I might have to leave the party because it had ceased to be a force for good. Also in March 2018 Jeremy acknowledged the problem of antisemitism in the party and said that it wasn't a matter of 'simply a few bad apples'. In April 2018 the party said that it would settle the 'vast majority' of outstanding antisemitism cases by the end of July 2018

I wrote to Jeremy to plead with him to deal with the problem in March 2018, but still at that stage there was the hope that he (and the party in general) might do so, as he had made the recent

bad apples statement. I told myself that I would stay for the time being, but that I would leave in August 2018 if the promise to settle the 'vast majority' of outstanding antisemitism cases by the end of July wasn't acted on. I then ended up Leaving earlier (July 2018) because it was clear that things were getting worse rather than better and I couldn't live with myself any longer if I remained a member.
Best wishes,
Russell

Dany Louise

Hi Judith,
Just to let you know that the gap is even bigger than you think - my letter is dated 13th Feb 2019! However I would hazard a guess that people didn't resign at the beginning of 2017 because they were working towards the general election - and perhaps (from my perspective) they weren't aware of exactly how appalling the situation was in the June 2017 election. Also I don't think at that time that the Corbynistas had total control of the party mechanisms and therefore they/we still had hope that having brought it to the attention of senior management, it would be properly addressed.
For example, I know I still had hope after the Enough is Enough protest in March 2018 and the

following debate in Parliament, that AS wouldn't be ignored, or denied, and that these events would galvanise the Party into taking it seriously. I know I was aware of discussion which hadn't yet tipped into "the Labour Party is now a lost cause" mode.
Hope that helps,
Dany

Joe Goldberg
I suspect they went quietly. I think you left immediately, or after Brexit. And then 2017 is General Election.
Joe Goldberg

Joan Ryan
Dear Judith
This would be my explanation:
The main criticism of Corbyn from Labour moderates throughout the first two years of his leadership was that he was unelectable. But the closely fought election in 2017 undermined that critique. We should have been saying at the outset that Corbyn's hard-left project was morally wrong. That his hatred of Israel was repugnant. And that his tolerance of antisemitism – his past associations with Holocaust-deniers, Jew-haters

and terrorist-sympathisers – made him unfit to be Britain's Prime Minister. In short, our critique should have been rooted in a fear of what he would do in power, not a fear that he wouldn't be able to attain it.

Joan

Warren Morgan

Dear Judith,

I can only speak to the reasons behind the timing of my resignation, which was very much aligned firstly with advice from JLM but principally around the resignation of Luciana Berger in February 2018, a few weeks before the Enough Is Enough demonstration in Parliament Square.

I think many people were waiting to see what actions were being taken if any to address the situation, and by February/March of last year it became clear nothing would be done.

Regards,

Warren

Allan Barclay

Hi. Judith

I struggled with Corbyn being elected in 2015 but as a lifelong member of the Labour Party and as a Democrat I accepted the results of the 2015 election. My problems with Corbyn was the many rumours regarding his past with his links to

terrorists and the stories regarding antisemitism, racism etc.
I think the gap may be due to the fact like me most Labour stalwarts were willing to give him a chance. Also during that time the PLP were up in arms against him but Momentum and Unite stood by him; they turned the tables on the PLP and a quick leadership election pursued within the LP and he won easily. Then when 2017 came he came close to winning, or so Unite and Momentum claimed; but he did gain ground against the Tory Party so his popularity increased. Corbyn is lucky because of the support he has enjoyed and that his only real opposition was Mrs May, who was weak and feeble not strong and stable, but I am sure his luck will run out shortly.
Kind regards
Allan

Merilyn Davies
Hi Judith,
People hung on for as long as they could, hoping it would change, that Labour would do as it promised and fix the problems it had with antisemitism.
After two years it became obvious there was no fix, or if there were, Labour didn't want to find it and so people began to leave - some hung on to the NEC elections, some to the Enough is Enough rally, but gradually, and at whichever point we chose as individuals to leave, we all knew we had

to stand up and be counted, to be louder, and on the right side of history.
Basically, people had hope. And also love for their party, the friends they had made there, the family it had become. You forgive a lot of your family, you try to make excuses or emphasise good points, and it takes time to realise that family is abusive, damaging to your mental health, and then still more time to pluck up the courage to leave. I tried three times to leave but was talked back. In the end I left in a way which meant I couldn't go back - a very public and angry resignation on Twitter - because I knew if I didn't do it that way I'd never be able to.
Hope that helps
M

Jason Fojtik
Dear Judith,
Just so you know, after resigning from the Labour Party I was re-elected as an independent councillor and continue to serve with my labour values that were passed down by my parents and grandparents rather than the current Corbyn leadership that do not.
Ironically, even after leaving the party, I wish it no harm as I now have no political home. And I assure you it's a lonely existence to have to endure.
Good luck and best wishes,
Jason

Bridget Prentice

Dear Judith,

That is interesting that there is a gap between the first and second letters. I don't know the reason for that but I can offer some suggestions.

First, many people may have resigned without writing a letter. Or at least without making it public.

Second, Corbyn won a leadership election in September 2016 and I suspect many people felt they had to accept that and see if they could work from within. Then there was a General Election in 2017 and I would surmise most Labour Party members would have put these issues aside while they campaigned. I don't think that is the case anymore, but in 2017 it may well have been.

Finally, the antisemitic trolls etc seemed to increase rather than decrease despite the leadership saying they were doing something about it. I think that, along with Brexit and people beginning to recognise just how poor a leader Jeremy Corbyn was, things came together for people by 2018 and they decided individually that enough was enough.

I hope that helps. I'd be interested to hear if others have other views as to why it happened in this way.

Looking forward to the finished product.

Kind regards

Bridget

18th November 2019

WHAT I WISH I HAD KNOWN

Dr Daniel Allington

Senior Lecturer Social and Cultural Artificial Intelligence, Kings College London

Deputy Editor Journal of Contemporary Antisemitism

18 November 2019

I resigned from the Labour Party on 13 April 2017. As I informed my local constituency branch, I did so because of the National Constitutional Committee's failure to take meaningful action against Ken Livingstone over his inflammatory remarks about Zionism. 'If the Party can't bring itself to expel him,' I wrote, 'then I no longer feel that sending it money is the morally right thing to do.' And so I cancelled my direct debit. But there was so much else I should have said – and so much sooner – if only I had known.

It's worth remembering how wrong Livingstone was – and I don't mean just factually, but morally too. Adolf Hitler did not support Zionism. He did not support it in 1932, as Livingstone claimed; indeed, he did not support it ever. Like every serious antisemite, Hitler was utterly opposed to Zionism, his antizionism forcefully and unambiguously expressed in *Mein Kampf*. But Livingstone's assertion was no mere matter of historical ignorance. After all, he had first given voice to his views on the subject not in a discussion of twentieth century history, but in defence of a Labour MP who had endorsed the idea that Jews should be expelled from Israel. His point appeared to be that proposing the destruction of the world's only Jewish state could not be such a bad thing if Hitler, murderer of six million Jews, had supported its creation. In making it, he defended not only the MP in question, but also those Marxist-Leninists for whom belief in the unique evil of Zionism had become an article of faith of the sort that belief in the unique evil of Jewry had always been for Nazis. And this was surely why he persisted in his error, even after that error had been pointed out by multiple historians. Because those were the same Marxist-Leninists with whom he had fraternised for decades.

Why, then, did Labour let him off? At the time, I believed that the answer was nepotism: Livingstone was a longstanding ally of Jeremy Corbyn, and, as such, was now officially entitled to do whatever he wished. Unforeseen circumstances had propelled his pal into the leadership of the Labour Party, and – from the point of view of their socialist old boys' network – it was time for the clique to inherit the earth.

That analysis still holds up, so far as it goes, but now it seems very incomplete. It wasn't that a party grandee *just happened* to be a spiteful old bore with a track record of ignorant and offensive remarks about the Holocaust, nor that the grandee in question had been given the same half-hearted slap on the wrist that he would likely have received had he engaged in any other misbehaviour short of an actual crime. It was that a worldview infected by stereotypes, conspiracy theories, and knee-jerk condemnation of those countries which had declined to ally themselves with the Soviet Union or the People's Republic of China had by that point become dominant across much of the British left, including within the formerly pro-Zionist and anti-communist Labour Party. In such a context, antisemitism – under the guise of antizionism – was able to reinvent itself not only as compatible with leftism, but as a species of leftism in its own right. And how could a former mayor be expelled for that?

I wasn't alone in my failure to grasp the extent of this ideological corruption. Because the Labour Party had for so long been led by pragmatists, very few people had noticed the rise of the crank left. But across the rank and file of the party, there were now vast numbers of self-identified 'socialists' the pillars of whose ideology were anti-capitalism, anti-Americanism, and virtually unconditional support for the enemies of Israel. Layer of wreaths, defender of murals, Corbyn articulated widely-held sentiments when he described hate preacher and blood libeller Raed Salah as an 'honoured citizen' and 'voice of the Palestinians', and declared – in his regular column in Britain's only communist daily newspaper, where else? – that 'it's time that Western governments stood up to the Zionist lobby' and ceased to categorise people of Salah's stripe as antisemitic. But I hadn't noticed, and nor had most other people. Even today, the average person would struggle to believe the truth.

What we have come to call Corbynism was many years in the making – and not only by the Corbyns and the Livingstones of this world, but also by those who have seen them as essentially virtuous.

If elected, Corbyn will be to the United Kingdom as he has been to the Labour Party: the figurehead of a self-righteous mob willing to tolerate Jews on its turf only on condition that they do nothing to challenge its hateful and regressive beliefs. And so it shall be for all groups – including Muslims, whose side the crank left takes only when ideologically convenient (let no one forget that Corbyn opposed military action against the genocidaires of Syria and former Yugoslavia).

The signs were there long before the spring of 2017, but only for those with the wit to read them. I'm glad that I left – but I regret that it took me so long.

What Is Institutional Antisemitism?

Dr Eve Garrard

moral philosopher with a special interest in issues to do with evil, the Holocaust, and forgiveness. She was Senior Lecturer in the Centre for Professional Ethics at Keele University, and is now an Honorary Research Fellow in the Department of Philosophy at Manchester University.

We all know what antisemitism is: it's a form of racism - racism against Jews. It usually (though not always, as we shall see) involves hatred or contempt or some other marked form of hostile feeling towards Jews, and it standardly issues forth in prejudiced, bigoted, discriminatory forms of behaviour, behaviour which treats Jews unfairly, and disadvantages them compared to members of other racial or religious groups. At its mildest it may involve jokes or snide remarks or a little sneering about Jews[1]; at its worst antisemitism commits genocide. (This latter possibility was within living memory a nightmare reality. In various parts of the world it's still half-secretly sympathised with, by rather more people than most Jews can feel entirely comfortable about. It's what gives antisemitism its especially

---

1 Not all jokes about Jews are antisemitic; if they were, and were consequently rejected, then Jewish comedians could lose half their material overnight.

dark and sinister aura.)
Antisemitism comes in many different forms and guises. One of these has fairly recently acquired its own label: institutional antisemitism. When an institution or organisation – a business, say, or a public service or a political party or a university or a union or a professional society – engages in customs or practices or policies which discriminate against Jews, for no good reason, then its behaviour is institutionally antisemitic.[2] Why do we need the special concept of institutional antisemitism to mark off this form of antisemitism from other, more familiar, ones? Why not just call them all antisemitism? There are two main reasons for this: one is that standardly` antisemitism is a matter of individuals, singly or in groups, knowingly and deliberately discriminating against Jews. But in cases of institutional antisemitism it's features of

---

2 The concept of institutional racism in general became quite widely used after the publication of the MacPherson Report into the murder of Stephen Lawrence, in which the police were charged with being institutionally racist in their handling of that crime. And a similar concept is available for cases of sexism, in which procedures and policies which disadvantage women without any adequate justification will amount to cases of institutional sexism, even though no feelings of hostility or contempt towards women need be involved.

the overall institution which create the discriminatory impact; no individual member of the institution need have deliberately and knowingly singled out Jews for unfair treatment, although Jews would have nonetheless been unfairly treated. Suppose, for example, there was an organisation some of whose employees were Jewish, which held all its staff meetings, where important policies were decided, and where promotions and appointments were discussed, on Saturday mornings. No observant Jews would be able to attend these meetings, and this might seriously diminish their chances of taking full part in the life of the organisation, and of taking on senior work within it. If this practice were maintained even after it was pointed out what its effects on Jewish members of staff would be, then this would be a case of institutional antisemitism.

There is a second, and perhaps even more notable, feature of institutional antisemitism which distinguishes it from what we might call the classic cases of antisemitism, in which the antisemite is filled with hatred and contempt for Jews, and acts in conformity with those feelings. However in institutional antisemitism, no hatred or disdain, indeed no particularly hostile feelings at all, need be involved. (They *may* be involved, but they *needn't* be.) Because the more ordinary cases of antisemitism do very frequently stem from strongly hostile feelings, people often think that where there is no hatred, there can be no antisemitism. But this does not follow: if there is behaviour which discriminates against Jews, which treats them unfairly compared to other people, without any good reason, then this is antisemitic behaviour. It's a form of antisemitism which does not depend on feelings at all, which is why people who are charged with participating in institutional antisemitism often refuse to accept the charge, on the grounds that they have no hostile feelings towards Jews. Even where this denial of hostility is true (which not always the case), it's the discriminatory effect, which does not depend on hostile feelings, that makes the behaviour or policy institutionally antisemitic.

This is a quite general point about the nature of discrimination, and it applies to discrimination against persons of colour as well as against Jews, and for that matter it also applies to discrimination against women and to discrimination on the basis of class.

Discrimination isn't always a matter of strong and hostile feelings. Think of a school which has a policy of discouraging pupils of colour, or girls, or children from a working-class background, from applying to top universities, on the (misplaced) grounds that they probably won't be accepted for them, and that they will be hurt and damaged by the rejection, and in any case will (supposedly) be more comfortable in a less academically demanding environment. (All of these things have happened in the past, and may still be happening in some places in this country now.) The teachers carrying out such practices may have feelings towards their pupils which are indulgent and protective rather than strongly hostile. But the practice is institutionally racist (or sexist, or imbued with class prejudice) all the same, since it depends on derogatory stereotypes of the abilities of members of the groups in question – people of colour, women, members of the working-class. The practice systematically and unfairly disadvantages the pupils affected by it, without good reason.

This 'without good reason' clause is of the first importance here. This is because there are some cases where members of one racial group do get disadvantaged compared to members of other groups, but if there's a good reason for this, then no racism, institutional or otherwise, need be involved. For example, consider a health clinic with a limited budget which has to decide whether to provide a screening programme for disease A (quite painful and disfiguring, but self-limiting after about three months), or one for disease B (curable if treated early, but potentially lethal if not). The catchment area for the clinic contains members of two fairly distinct racial groups, which I'll call with striking originality Group A* and Group B*. Members of Group A* are for broadly genetic reasons especially susceptible to disease A, and members of Group

B* are for broadly genetic reasons especially susceptible to disease B. The clinic decides to use its funds to screen for disease B, because unlike disease A it's life-threatening. But members of Group A* complain that they're being unfairly disadvantaged, and hence racially discriminated against. They acknowledge that no-one is displaying, or indeed feeling, any hostile attitudes towards them, but claim that this is nonetheless a case of institutional racism. But the clinic (rightly) replies that there's no unfairness taking place, that there's a good reason for disadvantaging A* people, which is that the alternative would be so much worse for B* people. There's a good reason for the differential treatment, and so no racism, institutional or otherwise, is involved.

One of the most troubled areas of dispute about antisemitism concerns attitudes and behaviour towards Israel, the world's only Jewish state, whose existence is supported by a very large majority of the world's Jews.

It's often claimed, quite truthfully, that criticism of Israel isn't the same as antisemitism. Such criticism needn't be antisemitic, and that's a fact. However that doesn't rule out the possibility that in some cases it can be, and indeed actually is, genuinely antisemitic, and that's a fact too. So what makes the difference? Those who support proposals to boycott Israel[3] - its products, its projects, its institutions and its personnel - on account of its various (alleged) misdeeds, often want to say that no antisemitism is involved, since they feel no hostility towards Jews, only towards the activities, and in some cases the existence, of the Jewish state.

Sometimes these no-hatred claims are manifestly false, since the hostility is palpable and venomous, especially of course online. In other cases, however, it may be true that no feelings of personal hatred or contempt are in play. But as we have seen, this doesn't rule out the possibility of institutional antisemitism, since that's not primarily a matter of feelings at all, it's a matter of policies and practices which unfairly disadvantage Jews in comparison to other group

Where boycotters justify their project by reference to Israel's (supposed) violations of human rights, then even where these criticisms are true, as they sometimes but not always are, we need to look at how other groups get treated. Do boycotters show any similar objections to, or engage in campaigns to boycott, other countries which have comparable, and often far worse, problems? In the Middle East alone, there are many countries whose violations of human rights

3 The boycott project is often referred to by its supporters as BDS, standing for boycott, divestment, and sanctions.

are far, far greater than those of Israel, such as Syria, Libya, Saudi Arabia, Iran, and Yemen, but there's a remarkable absence of campaigns by BDS supporters to boycott those states.

If the reason for singling out Israel is supposed to be that it's an occupying power, are there plans to boycott Turkey, China, Morocco, Russia, all also occupying powers? If the problem is claimed to be that Israel is an objectionably ethno-religious state, are there calls to boycott other ethno-religious states such as Iran, Saudi Arabia, Mauretania, or Pakistan? (Pakistan is a particularly illuminating case, since it achieved independence at about the same time as Israel did, but with far, far more blood being shed as it wrenched itself away from India to set up as an Islamic state.)

The answer to all these questions is of course no. It's hard to see what good reason there can be for singling out Israel for adverse treatment, up to and including calls for its annihilation. (It isn't unfortunately hard to identify some very bad reasons indeed.)

In the absence of any adequate justification for singling out Israel, alone among the nations, for boycott, divestment and sanctions, it seems that organisations which adopt the boycott policy provide us with striking examples of institutional antisemitism.

Institutional antisemitism is not in itself any worse than other forms of that most ancient of prejudices. But it isn't any better, either, and shouldn't be regarded as a less injurious or more excusable aspect of the sorry history of racism against Jews.

ANTISEMITISM AND MISOGYNY IN THE LABOUR PARTY

Dr David Hirsh
Senior Lecturer in Sociology, Goldsmiths, University of London
Author of Contemporary Left Antisemitism

The Labour Party took a year finally to suspend a party member who abused two MPs, Ruth Smeeth and Dame Margaret Hodge, as 'a couple of s**t-stirring c*m buckets bought and paid for by Israel'. It only acted after the case was reported in the press.

Something happens at the intersection of antisemitism and misogyny which creates a fury greater than the sum of its parts and which drips with sexual violence.

The party only suspended this abuser after the case was leaked to the Sunday Times, which reported that Thomas Gardiner, 'a Corbyn ally and the powerful chief of Labour's governance and legal unit', frustrated efforts by a member of his staff to fast-track the investigation of this incident. He didn't want this incident to jump the queue. No special favours for Ruth and Margaret. Do they think they're something special?

Ruth Smeeth WhatsApped Jeremy Corbyn personally to ask him what he was going to do about this. She got two ticks but no response. And her mother had to read it in the paper over her cornflakes on a Sunday morning. And Margaret Hodge's grandchildren saw it too.

Labour Party staff members have had to turn whistle-blower. One of them secretly leaked emails to the Sunday Times which proved that the Labour machine was unwilling to deal with the hundreds of cases of explicit antisemitism which had been reported to it.

The evidence provided by the whistle-blowers also demonstrated that while the leader of the party said that dealing with these cases was not his job, his private office took a keen interest. It intervened in the process to help some of Corbyn's allies who had allowed their antisemitism to slip into the open.

Indeed, even as recently as the Johnson v Corbyn election debate, Jeremy Corbyn stated, untruthfully, that all of the cases of antisemitism in the party had been investigated.

And then a number of Labour staffers talked to John Ware when he made his Panorama documentary, which showed how hard the Labour Party machine had worked to maintain a safe space for the antisemitism of Corbyn's allies in the party.

We knew that the Labour machine would turn ferociously against the whistle-blowers within its own staff. Institutional racism requires a strict policing of the boundaries between 'inside' and 'outside'. What passes for normal 'inside' must be kept separate from the outside world where it would easily be recognised as racist.

Populism always turns on the messengers in order to avoid hearing the message. It brands them 'enemies of the people' instead of listening to what they say.

I myself am still banned from the email discussions within my own trade union, after having published some of the antisemitic material there which was considered legitimate by the internal union culture. That was in 2008, that is so far, an eleven-year sentence.

Everybody who does get expelled from Labour for antisemitism joins a growing mob of other furious, resentful individuals. Some of them come straight back in through what Joan Ryan calls the revolving door. And they accuse Corbyn of bending to Zionist power; and they nurture a growing faction of comrades still in the party who support them. And they will blame the Jews who opposed antisemitism for Labour's ultimate failure to deliver utopia.

Every expulsion and every protest against antisemitism is greeted with howls of fresh antisemitic abuse. Look at the vileness of the comments which attach to any article or tweet which exposes or protests against antisemitism.

And in the end, expulsions significantly miss the point. The antisemitism that is recognisable to everybody is only a side-effect of the hidden and deep political problem on the left.

Like a black hole, you cannot see institutional antisemitism. Remember Katie Bouman's ground breaking image of a black hole? The un-observable object showed us its shape only by allowing us to see what it causes around itself. Google her name and you find this in some disgusting corner of the web: "Don't really have any evidence besides she looks Jewish, went to (((Harvard))), and last name is (((Bouman))). F*****g Zio-Media. Any goats have any confirmation that she is an oven-dodger?" There is something about the success of an intelligent and tough Jewish woman which is unendurable to today's antisemtic misogynist.
Labour's problem is not the antisemitic apples but the institutional barrel which turns them bad. Today's British left thinks it understands institutional racism but with its own antisemitism it forgets everything it knows. Like anybody who is in denial, the Labour movement keeps imagining it can fix itself. The beginning of the way out is to admit that it has a problem. But it won't and it can't.
The Jewish community still loves Labour, or it loves what Labour once was, somewhere deep in its heart; it remembers that its parents and grandparents were poor and were refugees; some worked their way out, but many of us are still working hard to live, like anybody else.
Jews are itching to help heal Labour, but Labour needs to ask for their help. And Labour won't.

Because the Labour we love is the Labour of our nostalgic dreams; it existed in some ways and at some times; but for the moment it is gone. It is replaced by the socialism of our nightmares; the socialism which held us responsible for capitalism; the socialism from which our grandparents fled; the socialism of the gulag. This socialism is the one which after embracing us as its activists and intellectuals, turned on us in resentful fury, saying we weren't part of the movement, we were rootless and cosmopolitan, loyal only to our own kind; the socialism which thought of us as too clever by half; which said that we betrayed 'the people', as though we were not ourselves part of 'the people'.

And now British socialism makes Jews symbolic of imperialism, apartheid and racism. It makes them again, the embodiment of everything to be feared, uncovered and rooted out. And sexism, which was never fully rooted out of the left, oozes from the dark corners of the new macho totalitarian thinking too. And the two vilenesses find each other and they come together and they form hateful unions which are worse than the sum of their already frightening parts.

But it is significant that the current populist challenge to our democratic state and our democratic culture does not only come only from the left, it comes from the right too.

Populism generally responds to criticism of the tough guy 'voice of the people' by denouncing the critic as an enemy rather than by presenting reasons why they may be mistaken. In that context, the sexist belittling of women in public life is becoming more common and more bitter. It is also in the context of the new populism that charges of antisemitism are more frequently met by counter-allegations of the Jewish or Zionist bad faith of the person who articulates the charges, than with an examination of the argument or the evidence they put forward. It is no surprise, then, that people who are both Jewish and female have had to deal with a lot of hostility.

But something happens at the intersection of antisemitism and misogyny which is even more than the addition of one kind of vileness to the other. Women who have opposed antisemitism have not only been subjected to a huge quantity of abuse. There has also been a particular quality of abuse, both misogynistic and antisemitic, which is more than a simple addition of the two.

THE INTERSECTION OF ANTISEMITISM AND MISOGYNY IN THE LABOUR PARTY

Dr Lesley Klaff

Senior Lecturer in Law, Sheffield Hallam University
Editor, Journal of Contemporary Antisemitism

There is nothing new about misogyny in politics. Defined as "dislike of, contempt for, or ingrained prejudice against women", misogyny is said to consistently feature in politics because of male resentment against women taking positions of political power. Thus, when Theresa May was Prime Minister she was nicknamed "Maybot" and repeatedly portrayed in cartoons as a robot-like creature who lacked all imagination and judgment. The cartoons were vicious in other ways, too: she was either characterised as an ugly figure, dripping in blood and guts, or as brainlessly obeying the orders of Jean-Claude Juncker. In America, when Hillary Clinton's memoir about the 2016 presidential election was published, she ended up on the receiving end of the kind of vitriol that no other failed presidential candidate has ever experienced, including those who have written books about their disappointed hopes. With respect to the situation in Britain, Dawn Butler, Labour's Shadow Minister for Women and Equalities, acknowledged in April 2018 that "more needs to be done to tackle the vile abuse and misogyny that I and other women MPs have faced once elected..."

Not only are women politicians vulnerable to misogynistic abuse, but Jewish politicians are vulnerable to antisemitic abuse. Who can forget those posters put out by the Labour Party in the run-up to the 2005 general election which depicted the faces of the Conservative Party leader Michael Howard and the Shadow Chancellor Oliver Letwin, who are Jewish, superimposed upon flying pigs? The slogan was "The Day Tory Sums Add Up" and the poster illustrated the hyperbolic figure of speech "when pigs fly" to indicate that it would never happen. Given that there is no animal as deeply disgusting to Jewish sensitivities as the pig, and given the economic libel that Jews financially exploit non-Jews and cannot be trusted, the poster was naturally criticised for its antisemitism. A second poster which depicted Michael Howard as a Dracula figure swinging a hypnotic watch was said by *The Jewish Chronicle* to be reminiscent of fictional Jewish, criminal characters, such as the moneylender Shylock from Shakespeare's *Merchant of Venice* and the master pickpocket, Fagin, from Charles Dickins' *Oliver Twist*. To the credit of the Labour Party at that time, the posters were withdrawn, along with the publication of an unreserved apology. More recently, the former speaker of the House of Commons, John Bercow disclosed that a constituent told him "you know, if I had my way, people like you, *Berkoff,* wouldn't be in this place," by which he apparently meant that he did not think that Jews should serve in Parliament. Zac Goldsmith, Ed Miliband and Lord Mann, to name but three, have reportedly also been recent victims of antisemitic abuse. Indeed, Lord Mann, who is not Jewish but who has a record of speaking out against antisemitism in the Labour Party and elsewhere, only had to make a mere appearance on the BBC programme *Question Time* in February 2018 to be accused of being "in the pay of the Israeli government."

Since Jeremy Corbyn became leader of the Labour Party, a new, hybrid type of abuse combining antisemitism and misogyny has been directed at Jewish female politicians who have voiced concerns about antisemitism in the Labour Party. The victims of this so-called *intersectional* abuse have included Luciana Berger, Ruth Smeeth, Dame Margaret Hodge and Dame Louise Ellman, as well as non-Jewish female politicians who have stood by them, such as Stella Creasey and Jess Phillips. Abuse that combines both antisemitism and misogyny is not only qualitatively different from either one on its own, but is also infinitely worse in its combined contempt and loathing for women and Jews.

Take, for example, the abuse of Ruth Smeeth and Dame Margaret Hodge, who were accused by a Labour Party member of being "a couple of s**t-stirring c*m buckets bought and paid for by Israel."

This short statement is vitriolic. It is resentful of Jews and resentful of women and is especially resentful of Jewish women politicians. This is because both antisemitism and misogyny involve notions of power, control and domination, and Jewish women are at the intersection of both. Notions of power, control and domination are even more concentrated in the case of Jewish women who hold political power.

In order to illustrate the unique nature of the resentment that occurs at the intersection of antisemitism and misogyny, let us return to the example of misogynistic abuse directed at Hillary Clinton. The most overwhelming sentiment about her and her book was that she just needed to go away. This was summed up by the *New York Times*, which asked, "What's to be done about Hillary Clinton, the woman who won't go away?", by an issue of *Vanity Fair,* which ran an article headlined, "Can Hillary Clinton Please Go Quietly Into The Night?" and by an open editorial in New York's liberal tabloid, the *Daily News,* which implored, "Hey Hillary Clinton, shut the f**k up and go away." These sentiments were disparaging of Hillary Clinton but they clearly lacked the vitriol, the sexual violence, and the malice that exudes from the language used to abuse the Jewish Ruth Smeeth and Dame Margaret Hodge. Similarly, the misogynistic abuse directed at Theresa May was vicious and mocking but it had none of the rage, malice or violence to be found in the following abusive tweet by a Labour Party member directed at Ruth Smeeth in early 2018: "The gallows would be a fine and fitting place for this dyke piece of yid s**t to swing from." This tweet debased and demeaned her. The word "dyke" in this context was presumably being used in its original form: as a homophobic and misogynistic slur. Moreover, the reference to her swinging from the gallows was violent. Smeeth reported to the House of Commons in April 2018 that she experienced this tweet as threatening. It undermined her sense of personal security.

The only expressions of violence in the case of Theresa May's misogynistic abuse, on the other hand, appear to have been in the expression of certain lynch mob sentiments expressed by her own party members, such as when one of them said she should bring a noose to the meeting of the backbenchers 1922 committee.

In fact, the violence that lies at the intersection of antisemitism and misogyny is particularly noteworthy. Luciana Berger, Ruth Smeeth and Dame Margaret Hodge told the 2018 *Sara Conference Against Misogyny and Antisemitism,* which was organised and hosted by the Antisemitism Policy Trust in partnership with the Community Security Trust, that they received repeated rape threats by means of emails and social media messages. These were invariably coupled with misogynistic and sexually violent references to their Jewishness, such as "Zionist bitch" or, more frequently, "Zionist c**t." Feminists have argued that words like "bitch" and "c**t act to reinforce a dehumanisation of women by reducing them to mere body parts. What is curious is that it was *only* in the case of Jewish women politicians that such dehumanisation was thought to be appropriate. It was thought to be appropriate, moreover, by members of Corbyn's Labour Party simply because these Jewish women politicians had complained about the Party's antisemitism. There was a time when the only negative stereotype about Jewish women that was likely to be levelled at politicians was the Jewish American Princess or JAP stereotype. This stereotype has been described as a combination of antisemitism and misogyny because it remodels the traditional antisemitic tropes into a female form: she is materialistic, money-grabbing, manipulative, shallow, crafty and ostentatious. Nevertheless, the stereotype was not often challenged and was, in fact, considered to be socially acceptable, even appearing in fictional works like *Marjorie Morningstar* by Herman Wouk and *Goodbye Columbus* by Philip Roth, as well as various 1980s films, such as *Private Benjamin* (1980) and *Dirty Dancing* (1987). These women were beautiful, sexually active, desirable, indulged in by their parents, and socially upwardly mobile. A report titled, "Hidden Hate: What Google Searches Tell Us About Antisemitism Today" published jointly

by the Antisemitism Policy Trust and the Community Security Trust in April 2019, stated that Jewish female politicians are the subject of more antisemitic searches than Jewish male politicians. The most common google searches about Luciana Berger reveal the influence of the JAP stereotype, but are relatively benign.
Since Jeremy Corbyn became leader of the Labour Party, however, Luciana Berger is more likely to be portrayed as a "Zionist bitch", a "Zionist c**t" or a "Zionist whore" than as a Jewish American Princess. For example, in September 2018 a hand-written letter delivered to her Wavertree constituency office in Liverpool began with,
"Hello Luciana, You nasty, stinking, lying, Zionist 'Jew-Bitch'"
And ended with
"Attached is correspondence of what Brother Lewis (sic) Farrakhan thinks about you stinking Jews. Have a good read, c**t..... And see you later!! Yeah!!!"
The letter was signed by people who described themselves as "Corbyn supporters." The ugly, destructive, and malicious emotions that are fed by the combination of misogyny and antisemitism are evident, even in this short extract.
It is apparent from the few examples offered here, and there are many more, that the abuse that occurs at the intersection of antisemitism and misogyny is qualitatively different from, and far worse than, either antisemitism or misogyny

alone. David Hirsh has summed it up well with the statement that this hybrid form of abuse is more than the sum of its equal parts.

It has, of course, caused immense harm to its victims because it has threatened their security and morale, and has overwhelmed them with its insults. More than that, it has harmed all those of us who care about the Labour Party: it has corrupted political discourse and shocked us with the Party's capacity for hatred. This is another reason why we have been forced out.

THAT LABOUR PARTY SPOKESMAN

Judith Ornstein

Whenever the media exposes antisemitism in the Labour Party, they also include a statement from the ubiquitous 'Labour Party Spokesman' who repeats, obfuscates, denies, and impugns character.
Since 2015, promises have failed to deliver and words haven't turned into actions, from 2016's Chakrabarti Inquiry whitewash until now, November 2019. Below are a few examples of the genre.

What the Labour Party spokesman has never said: that Labour has reflected; takes responsibility; is sorry about the people it has hurt and is putting its house in order right now.
If they had, the EHRC wouldn't be investigating them. Instead, because of antisemitism, thousands of traditional Labour members have reflected; realised this leadership doesn't speak for them; and left the party.
We should have heeded Howard Jacobson who warned that Jeremy Corbyn hasn't changed his mind for forty years.

In Nov 2019 JVL issued advice for Labour members facing the media. It's not a million miles from the tone of the Labour Party spokesman and suggests a possible close relationship. Here's an extract:

'Dealing with the media or aggressive attacks
If you are dealing with people who try to use antisemitism allegations to bury Labour and Corbyn give them no quarter

'Don't be apologetic.
'Go on to the offensive.
'Turn every question and allegation about antisemitism 'into a positive statement about the best of Labour's 'anti-discrimination, anti-fascist, pro-refugee past and 'its continued commitment to help *everyone* who is 'disadvantaged.
'Insist: "You have no basis for saying that! What 'particular policy do you object to, one you think that 'discriminates against Jews"'

Examples of the spokesman and compare to JVL advice

26/11/19 Jeremy Corbyn failed to apologise for Labour antisemitism four times in a TV interview with Andrew Neil.

11/7/19 The Guardian describes John Ware's harrowing Panorama documentary (BBC 10//7/19):

'Eight whistle-blowers have said how they felt fatally undermined by senior Labour bosses in their attempts to tackle antisemitism, alleging consistent interference in complaints and claiming that one key aide mocked their efforts.'

Embedded in the article is an example of Labour's vilification of whistle-blowers:

'Labour robustly denies any interference and said that "former disaffected employees sought the view of staff in the leader's office, which was complied with in good faith."'

15/7/19 'Corbyn under fire from staff and Labour peers over antisemitism'

'Jeremy Corbyn has come under renewed pressure as more than 100 former and current staff and another hundred Labour members and supporters challenged him to resign if he could not renew trust in Labour party's dealings with employees, and senior Labour peers offered to step in to overhaul its antisemitism complaints procedures.'

In the same news item:

'After the documentary aired on Wednesday, **a Labour party spokesperson said several of the whistle-blowers involved held political grudges against Corbyn**.

"These disaffected former officials include those who have always opposed Jeremy Corbyn's leadership, worked to actively undermine it, and have both personal and political axes to grind," the spokesman said. "It is simply untrue to say that there were any significant number of disagreements about what constituted antisemitism.

"Labour is taking decisive action against antisemitism, doubling the number of staff dedicated to dealing with complaints and cases. And since Jennie Formby became general secretary, the rate at which antisemitism cases have been dealt with has increased fourfold."'

There was widespread revulsion at Labour's spiteful attacks on brave and vulnerable young whistle-blowers.

13/7/19 The Guardian reported 'Whistle-blowers to sue Labour as antisemitism row deepens.'

13/7/19 The Times reported **'Labour has demanded that the BBC remove its Panorama documentary about antisemitism in the party from iPlayer.'**

The BBC stood by its programme and by John Ware who made it, refusing to comply.

1/11/19 the JC wrote that they understood John Ware was going to sue Labour over public statements criticising his reputation.

Martin Bright has written 'The latest management thinking suggests that badly-run organisations always treat whistle-blowers as a virus that needs to be eradicated rather than "good bacteria" to be encouraged. It would appear the Labour Party didn't get the memo' (JC 14/11/19).

27/8/18 a year before Panorama:

'Hundreds of complaints of alleged antisemitism against Labour members remain unaddressed and its internal investigation unit has all but collapsed, insiders say.

'Jeremy Corbyn has repeatedly promised to speed up the party's disciplinary process, most recently in a filmed apology for the hurt caused to British Jews this month.'

From the same article: **'A Labour spokesman said: "We have robust processes for dealing with complaints we receive."'**

20/11/19 The final example is an ITV debate. This time the Labour Party spokesman is Jeremy Corbyn, stating: 'I have taken action in my party where anyone has committed any antisemitic acts or made any antisemitic statements, they are either suspended or expelled from the party and we have investigated every single case.'

22/11/19 Buzzfeed's Hannah Al-Othman's headline revealed: 'More Labour Antisemitism Allegations Have Emerged After Jeremy Corbyn Said "Every Case" Had Been Investigated'

Hannah continues 'Peter Mason, the national secretary of the Jewish Labour Movement, claimed on Twitter that there were "at least 130 outstanding cases".'

Buzzfeed quotes an archetypal Labour spokesman obfuscation claiming that what Jeremy said isn't what Jeremy meant:

'A Labour source said that by "all cases have been investigated," Corbyn meant that they had passed the first stage of the process, but may still be subject to ongoing disciplinary proceedings.'

'Corbyn meant' has been a feature of his leadership. It feels like the Labour spokesman has a tendency to think that some of us don't understand English despite having lived in the UK for a very long time, or probably born here.

LIFE ON TWITTER
Gillian Lazarus
Warrior

When I try to recommend particular Twitter accounts which are activists against Labour antisemitism, I realize that there is an *embarrass de richesse*. There are accounts which educate and monitor and others which provide support and comfort. One can learn from Twitter about the political record of a dubious politician, journalist or spokesperson or about a Labour milieu in which antisemitism is allowed to flourish. Any online activist confronting antisemitism in the Labour party will be called unpleasant names, accused of crimes, become engaged with archly sarcastic adversaries or persistent, faux naïve questioners, who fall into the category of 'sealions'. All this has been my experience, besides which, my mugshot is occasionally displayed in a hostile environment, which is disconcerting. Yet there is so much warmth and friendship among what I might call comrades-in-arms, if the word comrades were not debased by being in constant use by the uncomradely.
Sometimes a simple 'like' or an encouraging word on Twitter is enough to restore faith in humanity despite the tsunami of ill will that has made life so difficult for many of us who once were supporters

of the Labour Party and now pray to be delivered out of their hands.

There are too many good Twitter accounts to list so here are just three. For a unique archive follow Corbyn in The Times@TimesCorbyn and when in need of irony go to Joo@JoosyJew and Milk Media@milkmedianewyor

TIMELINE

25/09/2010 Ed Miliband becomes leader of the Labour Party

07/05/2015 General Election - Conservative win with overall majority of 12

08/05/2015 Ed Miliband resigns

12/09/2015 Jeremy Corbyn becomes leader of the Labour Party. Registered supporters paying just £3 allowed to vote for the leader on a one member one vote basis. 84% of the new £3 voters back Corbyn

18/02/2016 Alex Chalmers resigns as co-chair of Oxford University Labour Club. Subsequently Baroness Royall's full report into allegations of antisemitism repressed

28/04/2016 Livingstone confronted by John Mann

23/06/2016 Brexit Referendum
24/06/2016 Cameron resigns

28/06/2016 Corbyn loses a motion of no confidence in him as leader. Labour MPs vote 197 to 40 against Corbyn. He rejects call to resign

30/06/2016 Chakrabarti Report published

13/07/2016 May becomes PM

24/09/2016 Corbyn sees off leadership challenge from Owen Smith and re-elected leader

08/06/2017 General Election - Labour Gain 30 seats and Conservatives lose overall majority but remain in Government

30/06/2017 Whitewashed published and premieres (www.whitewashed.co.uk)

26/03/2018 Enough is Enough rally outside Parliament

16/07/2018 68 Rabbis from across the denominations sign letter condemning Labour antisemitism

25/07/2018 The Jewish Chronicle, Jewish News and Jewish Telegraph all publish same headline stating that a government led by JC would be an 'existential threat to Jewish life'

22/02/2019 Nine MPs quit Labour citing the handling of antisemitism within the Party

28/05/2019 The Equalities and Human Rights Commission launch formal investigation into the Labour Party for institutional antisemitism

06/06/2019 Peterborough by-election – Labour's Karen Forbes elected even though she had endorsed antisemitic Facebook posts. Despite her subsequent apology, this demonstrates Labour's normalisation of antisemitism.

10/07/2019 Panorama: Is Labour Antisemitic?

16/07/2019 64 Labour Lords place advertisement accusing Corbyn of failing to deal with antisemitism in Labour

29/07/2019 General election announced for 12/12/19 – after this book goes to print

19/11/19 Corbyn claims on ITV that Labour has 'investigated every single case' of anti-Jewish racism. JLM sec Peter Mason writes on Twitter 'This is a lie' and backs it with evidence. (JC 20/11/19)

FORCED OUT
Meanings of abbreviations used in book

PLP: Parliamentary Labour Party
CLP: Constituency Labour Party
IHRA: International Holocaust Remembrance Alliance
NEC: National Executive Committee (of the Labour Party)
NCC: National Constitutional Committee (highest body in Labour for handling disciplinary issues)
JLC: Jewish Leadership Council
BoD: Board of Deputies (organisation representing many of the UK's Jewish community)
BNP: British National Party – far right, fascist
Canary: Hard Left media organisation supportive of Corbynism
Squawkbox: Hard Left media organisation supportive of Corbynism
EHRC: Equalities and Human Rights Commission
JLM: Jewish Labour Movement, affiliated to Labour for 100 years
JVL: Jewish Voice for Labour – antizionist splinter group set up 2017. Uncritical of Corbyn

Gaslighting: A form of psychological manipulation and abuse by which a person seeks to sow seeds of doubt in a targeted individual or group making them question their own memory, perception and sanity.

Dog whistle: The use of coded language that may appear benign to the general population but has an additional and often unpleasant and threatening resonance for a targeted individual or group.

Good Friday Agreement 1998: Brought an end to the Troubles (Northern Irish conflict)

Jeremy Corbyn

Some key facts

Before becoming Leader of the Labour Party:

2008 Appears regularly on Iranian Press TV paid £20000

2009 Describes representatives of Hamas as his 'friends' after inviting them to Parliament

2012 Supports antisemitic mural by Mear One

2013 States that 'Zionists ...having lived in this country for a very long time, probably all their lives, they don't understand English irony..'

2014 Lays a wreath in Tunisia honouring the perpetrators of the 1972 Munich Olympics massacre

LETTER FROM 68 RABBIS 16th July 2018 (first published in The Guardian)

As British rabbis, it is with great regret that we find it necessary to write, yet antisemitism within sections of the Labour party has become so severe and widespread that we must speak out with one Jewish voice.

The Labour party's leadership has chosen to ignore those who understand antisemitism the best, the Jewish community. By claiming to know what's good for our community, the Labour party's leadership have chosen to act in the most insulting and arrogant way.

It is not the Labour party's place to rewrite a definition of antisemitism accepted by the Crown Prosecution Service, College of Policing, the Scottish parliament, the Welsh assembly, the National Union of Students, and 124 local authorities, including scores of Labour-held councils, including Haringey and Greater Manchester – but above all else, accepted by the vast majority of Jewish people in Britain and globally.

On behalf of our communities, members and congregants, we urge the Labour party to listen to the Jewish community, adopt the full and unamended International Holocaust Remembrance Alliance (IHRA) definition of antisemitism including its examples, and like the organisations listed above, use the IHRA definition alone as their working definition of antisemitism.

Rabbi Dr Harvey Belovski Senior rabbi, Golders Green Synagogue, and vice-chair, Rabbinical Council of the United Synagogue

Rabbi Joseph Dweck Senior rabbi, Spanish and Portuguese Sephardi Community of the UK

Rabbi Laura Janner-Klausner Senior rabbi to Reform Judaism

Rabbi Nicky Liss Highgate Synagogue, and chair, Rabbinical Council of the United Synagogue

Rabbi Avrohom Pinter Principal of the Yesodey Hatorah schools

Rabbi Danny Rich Senior rabbi and chief executive of Liberal Judaism

Rabbi Jonathan Wittenberg Senior Rabbi to Masorti Judaism

Dayan Ivan Binstock Dayan (judge) of the London Beth Din, and senior rabbi, St John's Wood Synagogue

Rabbi Stuart Altshuler Belsize Square Synagogue

Rabbi Larry Becker Sukkat Shalom Reform Synagogue

Rabbi Yoni Birnbaum Hadley Wood Jewish Community, and executive, Rabbinical Council of the United Synagogue

Rabbi Yehuda Black Kenton United Synagogue

Rabbi Janet Burden Ealing Liberal Synagogue

Rabbi Baruch Davis Chigwell and Hainault Synagogue and past chair, Rabbinical Council of the United Synagogue

Rabbi Hadassah Davis Member of the Liberal Rabbinic Conference

Rabbi Colin Eimer Emeritus rabbi, Sha'arei Tsedek North London Reform Synagogue

Rabbi Daniel Epstein Cockfosters & North Southgate Synagogue

Rabbi Elchonon Feldman Senior rabbi, Bushey and District United Synagogue

Rabbi Yisroel Fine St Johns Wood Synagogue

Rabbi Paul Freedman Senior rabbi, Radlett Reform Synagogue

Rabbi Dr Moshe Freedman New West End Synagogue

Rabbi Ariel J Friedlander

Rabbi Yoni Golker Assistant rabbi, St John's Wood Synagogue

Rabbi Michael Harris Hampstead Synagogue

Rabbi Simon Harris Wembley Synagogue

Rabbi Frank Hellner Emeritus rabbi, Finchley Progressive Synagogue

Rabbi Jonny Hughes Radlett United Synagogue

Rabbi Geoffrey Hyman Rabbi, Ilford United Synagogue

Rabbi Dr Margaret Jacobi Birmingham Progressive Synagogue

Rabbi Richard Jacobi East London and Essex Liberal Synagogue

Cantor Zoe Jacobs Finchley Reform Synagogue

Rabbi Oliver Spike Joseph Elstree & Borehamwood Masorti Community
Rabbi Chaim Kanterovitz Senior Rabbi Borehamwood and Elstree Synagogue & Chair Vaad Harabonim Mizrachi UK
Rabbi Dov Kaplan Hampstead Garden Suburb Synagogue
Rabbi Yuval Keren Southgate Progressive Synagogue
Rabbi Michael Laitner Senior rabbi of United Synagogue Jewish Living, and assistant rabbi, Finchley Synagogue
Rabbi Jeremy Lawrence Senior rabbi, Finchley United Synagogue
Rabbi Barry Lerer Barnet Synagogue
Rabbi Judith Levitt
Rabbi Mendel Lew Stanmore & Canons Park Synagogue
Rabbi Shlomo Odze Associate rabbi, South Hampstead United Synagogue and vice-chair, Rabbinical Council of the United Synagogue
Rabbi Alan Mann
Rabbi Rodney Mariner Former rabbi, Belsize Square Synagogue
Rabbi David Mason Rabbi at Muswell Hill Synagogue and executive member, Rabbinical Council of the United Synagogue
Rabbi David Mitchell West London Synagogue
Rabbi Lea Mühlstein Northwood and Pinner Liberal Synagogue
Rabbi Rene Pfertzel Kingston Liberal Synagogue
Rabbi Hershel Rader Brighton and Hove Hebrew Congregation
Rabbi Dr Jonathan Romain Maidenhead Synagogue
Rabbi Michael Rosenfeld-Schueler Jewish chaplain, University of Oxford and Oxford Brookes
Rabbi Sylvia Rothschild Past chair of the Rabbinic Assembly of Reform Judaism
Rabbi Elli Tikvah Sarah Brighton and Hove Progressive Synagogue
Rabbi Dr J Shindler Executive director, Rabbinical Council of the United Synagogue
Rabbi Yitzchak Schochet Mill Hill Synagogue
Rabbi Irit Shillor Harlow Jewish Community

Rabbi Yitzchok Sufrin Enfield & Winchmore Hill United Synagogue
Rabbi Lee M Sunderland Romford & District Synagogue
Rabbi Dr Jackie Tabick Convener of the Beit Din, the Movement for Reform Judaism
Rabbi Roni Tabick New Stoke Newington Synagogue
Rabbi Sam Taylor Community rabbi, Western Marble Arch Synagogue
Rabbi Pete Tobias The Liberal Synagogue Elstree
Rabbi Alexander Tsykin Jewish chaplain, Bristol and Western Region
Rabbi Dr Martin van den Bergh Childwall Hebrew Congregation
Dayan Elimelech Vanzetta Rabbi, Ahavas Yisrael
Rabbi Charles Wallach Bournemouth Reform Synagogue
Rabbi Chaim Weiner Director of Masorti Europe and European Masorti Bet Din
Rabbi Roderick Young Former principal rabbi, Finchley Reform Synagogue
Rabbi Dr Andrea Zanardo Brighton and Hove Reform Synagogue

NOTE & MARK THIS ↓

INTERNATIONAL HOLOCAUST REMEMBRANCE ALLIANCE

Working Definition of Antisemitism

In the spirit of the Stockholm Declaration that states: "With humanity still scarred by ...antisemitism and xenophobia the international community shares a solemn responsibility to fight those evils" the committee on Antisemitism and Holocaust Denial called the IHRA Plenary in Budapest 2015 to adopt the following working definition of antisemitism.

On 26 May 2016, the Plenary in Bucharest decided to:

Adopt the following non-legally binding working definition of antisemitism:

"Antisemitism is a certain perception of Jews, which may be expressed as hatred toward Jews. Rhetorical and physical manifestations of antisemitism are directed toward Jewish or non-Jewish individuals and/or their property, toward Jewish community institutions and religious facilities."

To guide IHRA in its work, the following examples may serve as illustrations:

Manifestations might include the targeting of the state of Israel, conceived as a Jewish collectivity.

However, criticism of Israel similar to that leveled against any other country cannot be regarded as antisemitic. Antisemitism frequently charges Jews with conspiring to harm humanity, and it is often used to blame Jews for "why things go wrong." It is expressed in speech, writing, visual forms and action, and employs sinister stereotypes and negative character traits.

Contemporary examples of antisemitism in public life, the media, schools, the workplace, and in the religious sphere could, taking into account the overall context, include, but are not limited to: Calling for, aiding, or justifying the killing or harming of Jews in the name of a radical ideology or an extremist view of religion.

Making mendacious, dehumanizing, demonizing, or stereotypical allegations about Jews as such or the power of Jews as collective — such as, especially but not exclusively, the myth about a world Jewish conspiracy or of Jews controlling the media, economy, government or other societal institutions.

Accusing Jews as a people of being responsible for real or imagined wrongdoing committed by a single Jewish person or group, or even for acts committed by non-Jews.

Denying the fact, scope, mechanisms (e.g. gas chambers) or intentionality of the genocide of the Jewish people at the hands of National Socialist Germany and its supporters and accomplices during World War II (the Holocaust).

Accusing the Jews as a people, or Israel as a state, of inventing or exaggerating the Holocaust.

Accusing Jewish citizens of being more loyal to Israel, or to the alleged priorities of Jews worldwide, than to the interests of their own nations.

Denying the Jewish people their right to self-determination, e.g., by claiming that the existence of a State of Israel is a racist endeavor.

Applying double standards by requiring of it a behavior not expected or demanded of any other democratic nation.

Using the symbols and images associated with classic antisemitism (e.g., claims of Jews killing Jesus or blood libel) to characterize Israel or Israelis.

Drawing comparisons of contemporary Israeli policy to that of the Nazis.

Holding Jews collectively responsible for actions of the state of Israel.

Antisemitic acts are criminal when they are so defined by law (for example, denial of the Holocaust or distribution of antisemitic materials in some countries).

Criminal acts are antisemitic when the targets of attacks, whether they are people or property – such as buildings, schools, places of worship and cemeteries – are selected because they are, or are perceived to be, Jewish or linked to Jews.

Antisemitic discrimination is the denial to Jews of opportunities or services available to others and is illegal in many countries.

INTERNATIONAL HOLOCAUST REMEMBRANCE ALLIANCE
The examples

Statement by Experts of the UK Delegation to the IHRA on the Working Definition of Antisemitism 07.08.2018

Recently the work of the International Holocaust Remembrance Alliance (IHRA) has featured prominently in discourse concerning the troubling rise of antisemitic incidents in Britain. As members of the UK Delegation to the IHRA, we feel it is only appropriate for us to add our voice to this conversation in order to clarify what exactly the IHRA is and why its non-legally binding working definition of antisemitism, adopted on 26 May 2016, should be adopted widely, without amendment.

The IHRA exists to unite governments and experts from 31 Member Countries to strengthen, advance and promote Holocaust education, remembrance, and research worldwide. The UK has the proud distinction of being one of three founding members. As the only intergovernmental organisation mandated to focus solely on Holocaust-related issues including antisemitism, our network of experts was compelled in 2016 to address the global rise in antisemitic incidents by putting forth a clear 'gold-standard' definition of what contemporary antisemitism consists of.

The significance of this definition lies in the international cooperation that led to it. Not only was it drafted with input from many of the world's foremost experts on antisemitism, but it was unanimously approved by government representatives from all IHRA Member Countries. Gaining this level of international consensus was no easy feat, but antisemitism is a global phenomenon and so it was very important that we persevered in order to emerge with one common definition. As a result of this IHRA effort, there is not a western or an eastern definition of antisemitism; there is not a Jewish or non-Jewish definition – but an international definition.

Any 'modified' version of the IHRA definition that does not include all of its 11 examples is no longer the IHRA definition. Adding or removing language undermines the months of international diplomacy and academic rigour that enabled this definition to exist. If one organisation or institution can amend the wording to suit its own needs, then logically anyone else could do the same. We would once again revert to a world where antisemitism goes unaddressed simply because different entities cannot agree on what it is.

The real everyday threats to Jewish people and their communities demand coordinated international solutions. As members of the UK delegation to the IHRA, we are pleased that our work has provided an important tool to unite policymakers and stakeholders of different nationalities and ideologies in this urgent fight.

Signed,

Dr Gilly Carr
University of Cambridge
IHRA Academic Working Group

Dr Paula Cowan
University of the West of Scotland
IHRA Academic Working Group

Sir Ben Helfgott MBE
'45 Aid Society
IHRA Museums and Memorials Working Group

Karen Pollock MBE
Holocaust Educational Trust

Olivia Marks-Woldman
Holocaust Memorial Day Trust
IHRA Museums and Memorials Working Group

Alex Maws
Holocaust Educational Trust
IHRA Education Working Group

Michael Newman
The Association of Jewish Refugees (AJR)
IHRA Communication Working Group

INTERNATIONAL HOLOCAUST REMEMBRANCE ALLIANCE

Spelling of Antisemitism

The International Holocaust Remembrance Alliance (IHRA) would like to address the spelling of the term 'antisemitism', often rendered as 'anti-Semitism'. IHRA's concern is that the hyphenated spelling allows for the possibility of something called 'Semitism', which not only legitimizes a form of pseudo-scientific racial classification that was thoroughly discredited by association with Nazi ideology, but also divides the term, stripping it from its meaning of opposition and hatred toward Jews.
The philological term 'Semitic' referred to a family of languages originating in the Middle East whose descendant languages today are spoken by millions of people mostly across Western Asia and North Africa. Following this semantic logic, the conjunction of the prefix 'anti' with 'Semitism' indicates antisemitism as referring to all people who speak Semitic languages or to all those classified as 'Semites'. The term has, however, since its inception referred to prejudice against Jews alone.

In the mid-nineteenth century, the derived construct 'Semite' provided a category to classify humans based on racialist pseudo-science. At the same time the neologism 'antisemitism', coined by German journalist Wilhelm Marr in 1879 to designate anti-Jewish campaigns, was spread through use by anti-Jewish political movements and the general public. The modern term gained popularity in Germany and Europe incorporating traditional Christian anti-Judaism, political, social and economic anti-Jewish manifestations that arose during the Enlightenment in Europe, and a pseudo-scientific racial theory that culminated in Nazi ideology in the twentieth century. Although the historically new word only came into common usage in the nineteenth century, the term antisemitism is today used to describe and analyze past and present forms of opposition or hatred towards Jews. In German, French, Spanish and many other languages, the term was never hyphenated.

The unhyphenated spelling is favoured by many scholars and institutions in order to dispel the idea that there is an entity 'Semitism' which 'anti-Semitism' opposes. Antisemitism should be read as a unified term so that the meaning of the generic term for modern Jew-hatred is clear. At a time of increased violence and rhetoric aimed towards Jews, it is urgent that there is clarity and no room for confusion or obfuscation when dealing with antisemitism.

25th November 2019
Rabbi Ephraim Mirvis Chief Rabbi of the United Hebrew Congregations of the Commonwealth

The Times

Ephraim Mirvis: What will become of Jews in Britain if Labour forms the next government?
Elections should be a celebration of democracy. However, just weeks before we go to the polls, the overwhelming majority of British Jews are gripped by anxiety.
During the past few years, on my travels through the UK and further afield, one concern has been expressed to me more than any other. Of course, the threats of the far right and violent jihadism never go away, but the question I am now most frequently asked is: What will become of Jews and Judaism in Britain if the Labour Party forms the next government?
This anxiety is justified. Raising concerns about anti-Jewish racism in the context of a general election ranks among the most painful moments I have experienced since taking office. Convention dictates that the Chief Rabbi stays well away from party politics — and rightly so. However, challenging racism is not a matter of politics, it goes well beyond that. Wherever there is evidence of it, including in any of our political parties, it must be swiftly rooted out. Hateful

prejudice is always wrong, whoever the perpetrator, whoever the victim.

The Jewish community has endured the deep discomfort of being at the centre of national political attention for nearly four years. We have been treated by many as an irritant, as opposed to a minority community with genuine concerns. Some politicians have shown courage but too many have sat silent. We have learned the hard way that speaking out means that we will be demonised by faceless social media trolls and accused of being partisan or acting in bad faith by those who still think of this as an orchestrated political smear. Yet, I ask myself: should the victims of racism be silenced by the fear of yet further vilification?

Therefore, with the heaviest of hearts, I call upon the citizens of our great country to study what has been unfolding before our very eyes.

The Jewish community has watched with incredulity as supporters of the Labour leadership have hounded parliamentarians, members and even staff out of the party for challenging anti-Jewish racism. Even as they received threats, the response of the Labour leadership was utterly inadequate. We have endured quibbling and prevarication over whether the party should adopt the most widely accepted definition of antisemitism. Now we await the outcome of a formal investigation by the Equality and Human Rights Commission into whether discrimination by the party against Jews has become an institutional problem. And all of this while in opposition. What should we expect of them in government?

The way in which the leadership has dealt with anti-Jewish racism is incompatible with the British values of which we are so proud — of dignity and respect for all people. It has left many decent Labour members both Jewish and non-Jewish, ashamed of what has transpired.

The claims that the party is "doing everything" it reasonably can to tackle anti-Jewish racism and that it has "investigated every single case", are a mendacious fiction. According to the Jewish Labour Movement, there are at least 130 outstanding cases before the party, some dating back years, and thousands more have been reported but remain unresolved.

The party leadership have never understood that their failure is not just one of procedure, which can be remedied with additional staff or new processes. It is a failure to see this as a human problem rather than a political one. It is a failure of culture. It is a failure of leadership. A new poison – sanctioned from the top – has taken root in the Labour Party.

Many members of the Jewish community can hardly believe that this is the same party that they called their political home for more than a century. It can no longer claim to be the party of equality and anti-racism.

How far is too far? How complicit in prejudice would a leader of Her Majesty's opposition have to be to be considered unfit for office? Would associations with those who have incited hatred against Jews be enough? Would describing as "friends" those who endorse the murder of Jews be enough? It seems not.

It is not my place to tell any person how they should vote. I regret being in this situation at all. I simply pose the question: What will the result of this election say about the moral compass of our country? When December 12 arrives, I ask every person to vote with their conscience. Be in no doubt, the very soul of our nation is at stake.

Rabbi Ephraim Mirvis